MAY 0 7 2018

P9-AGD-640

NAPA COUNTY LIBRARY
580 COOMBS STREET
NAPA, CA 94559

# SWEET & SOUTHERN

## CLASSIC DESSERTS WITH A TWIST

### BEN MIMS

Photographs by Noah Fecks

**RIZZOLI**
NEW YORK

New York  Paris  London  Milan

First published in the United States of America in 2014
by Rizzoli International Publications, Inc.
300 Park Avenue South, New York, NY 10010
www.rizzoliusa.com

© Ben Mims
Photographs © Noah Fecks

All rights reserved. No part of this publication may be reproduced, stored in a retrieval
system, or transmitted in any form or by any means, electronic, mechanical, photocopying,
recording, or otherwise, without prior consent of the publishers.

2014 2015 2016 2017 / 10 9 8 7 6 5 4 3 2 1

Design by Lynne Yeamans
Printed in China

ISBN: 978-0-8478-4339-8
Library of Congress Call Number: 2014934985

# Contents

I GREW UP IN RURAL MISSISSIPPI. THE AREA WAS ISOLATED FROM MANY THINGS, BUT GREAT SWEETS WERE NOT among them. Layer cakes, pudding pies, fudge candies, fruit ice creams, and rich baked goods were part of my daily life. I ate them regularly and with fervor, never able to satisfy my sweet tooth. My mother Judy and her sister Barbara Jane were the same way. We'd always make time for something sweet while driving to the bank, to the grocery store, or to nearby Jackson to go shopping. Every Sunday at my grandmother Carol's house, we'd eat lunch after church and be treated to caramel or coconut layer cakes (pages 19 and 24) made by her neighbor. My mom made Pecan Pie (page 90) weekly, and Barbara Jane's Christmas tins of Pretzel-Peanut-Chocolate Candy (page 191), Crisp Oatmeal Raisin Cookies (page 175), and Cocoons (page 171) were the highlight of the whole family's holiday. Saturday mornings meant fluffy biscuits (page 118) or pancakes topped with a drizzle of syrup or locally made muscadine jelly.

As wonderful as those memories are, when I eat those sweets now, after years of living in New York City and San Francisco, I realize that the old-school southern levels of sweetness and richness are too intense for me—and I suspect they don't necessarily jive with most people's tastes for lighter, less sugary treats either. Over time, I've modernized many of my childhood-favorite recipes, so here you'll find a food coloring–free "Red Velvet" Cake featuring tart pomegranate juice (page 48), pecan pie made with a home-made natural "corn syrup" (page 90), and a simple bread pudding based on nutty skillet corn bread (page 124). They're not as sweet and rich as the traditional versions, but they certainly pack a punch. They are, unquestionably, desserts. They're balanced between the overly rich sweets of the Deep South and the barely sweetened New York City pastries and fruit-heavy West Coast–style desserts.

I've been working on striking that balance in my own recipes since my Mississippi days; my style was refined especially during my nearly five years at *Saveur* magazine, where I worked almost exclusively with the sweets and dessert recipes. I've come up with the most efficient and rewarding ways to achieve the best results, as well as how to use certain ingredients to my advantage. Just as cooks use salt and pepper in savory dishes, I use salt and vanilla extract in virtually all of my sweet recipes: Vanilla is the most familiar flavor to the American dessert palate, and the right amount of salt cuts through the sugar and fat in a dessert to balance its flavors. These ingredients offer a taste of the familiar to help bridge the taste gap that can occur when you eat a dessert. They're the backbones of the American dessert, and thus need to be there, if only in trace amounts, to bring the taste experience full circle.

While most of the dishes here are southern in spirit, many other recipes in this book have come about through my time at *Saveur*. These are recipes I've found to be strikingly similar throughout the world. Rice pudding, for example, is more or less the same in America as it is in Sweden and India, just spiced with different ingredients or using different kinds of rice. American sweet potato casserole bares a striking resemblance to Arabian spoon halva made with squash. Pecan pie is basically just British treacle tart with pecans added. And it's no wonder, since virtually all American desserts and baked goods descended from other parts of the world, mostly Europe. Seeing these similarities, I've morphed several traditional recipes from around the world to suit a southern palate—a Thanksgiving pie made in the style of *camotes*, Mexican sweet potatoes (page 70); a shredded phyllo pastry from the Middle East filled with pumpkin and soaked in a spiced syrup (page 101); and *cassata*, a traditional Sicilian dessert, here made with pecan marzipan and Bourbon-soaked cake, and topped with coconut (page 52). While these desserts range widely from simple to elaborate, their flavors remain clean and familiar, their elements balanced and their intensity moderate so you can enjoy a piece of cake, a slice of pie, or a cookie or two and not feel in need of a nap afterward. My philosophy is that having a little something sweet every day keeps overwhelming hunger pangs from capturing you and leaving you waking from a coma to find you've eaten half a peach pie.

With very few exceptions, the ingredients I use are natural—in other words, there's no bullshit added. Instead of packaged sweetened coconut, I use fresh-grated, and use the coconut's water to make my Coconut Cake (page 24). I'm also a realist and know that many people, novice and experienced bakers alike, take shortcuts from time to time because they're short on—well, time. And that's totally okay; I'm just here to let you know that if you have the inclination to avoid the shortcuts, the results will be proportionately more satisfying.

As you read this book, my hope is that whatever is daunting or intimidating to you about baking and pastry making becomes less so and that the information I have to share makes you feel more at ease. I aim to make recipes that are relatable and makeable, but also tweaked just enough to be interesting and new. Those lightbulb moments are what make learning fun, and I want your baking experiences to be occasions you look forward to, not dread. I'll gladly be your guide and show you it all really is as easy as pie.

—BEN MIMS

# Cakes

BLACK FOREST CAKE

BOURBON FRUITCAKE

CARROT SHEET CAKE

CANTALOUPE UPSIDE-DOWN CAKE

CARAMEL CAKE

CINNAMON-CHOCOLATE SPEKKUK

COCONUT CAKE

CINNAMON CRUMB CAKE

COCONUT-LIME CORNMEAL POUND CAKE

COFFEE TRES LECHES

CREAM CHEESE POUND CAKE

GERMAN CHOCOLATE CUPCAKES

HUMMINGBIRD CAKE

LEMON LAYER CAKE

LEMON-LIME SODA CAKE

MARBLED ORANGE-CHOCOLATE BUNDT CAKE

MISSISSIPPI MUD CAKE

RASPBERRY AND APPLE COFFEE CAKE

PEANUT BUTTER CUP SMITH ISLAND CAKE

"RED VELVET" CAKE

SOUR CREAM CHEESECAKE

SOUTHERN CASSATA

SWEET POTATO CAKE

SWEET & SMOKY SNACK CAKE

WALNUT SPICE CAKE

# Black Forest Cake

MAKES ONE 9-INCH LAYER CAKE

Growing up, I preferred candied chocolate-covered cherries to the very grown-up-looking cake topped with glowing red maraschinos, but however it comes, the combination of cherries and chocolate possesses an intoxicating allure I cannot resist.

This technique of stabilizing whipped cream with gelatin is a little more time-consuming than simply whipping cream, but it results in a perfectionist's dream frosting: It's easy to pipe and stays just where you put it. The cream frosting offsets the dense, deep chocolate of the devil's food cake perfectly, and a generous helping of sour cherries and hefty pour of kirsch (cherry brandy) balance the dark chocolate and airy, sweet frosting.

---

FOR THE CAKE:

8 ounces 60% dark chocolate, chopped

½ cup boiling water

2 cups all-purpose flour

1 teaspoon baking soda

¼ teaspoon kosher salt

1½ cups sugar

1 cup (2 sticks) unsalted butter, softened

1 teaspoon vanilla extract

4 large egg yolks

1 cup buttermilk

4 large egg whites

MAKE THE CAKE: Heat the oven to 350°F. Spray the insides of two 9-inch round cake pans evenly with baking spray. Put the chocolate in a small bowl and pour in the boiling water; let sit for 1 minute, then stir until smooth. In a medium-size bowl, whisk together the flour, baking soda, and salt.

Put 1¼ cups of the sugar, the butter, and vanilla in the bowl of a stand mixer fitted with the paddle attachment. Beat on medium-high speed until smooth. Add the egg yolks and beat until the mixture is completely incorporated and smooth. Add the dry ingredients alternately with the buttermilk and chocolate, and beat on low speed until the batter is smooth. In a separate bowl, whisk the egg whites and the remaining ¼ cup sugar until stiff peaks form; add to the batter and fold until smooth. Divide the batter between the prepared pans and smooth the tops with a rubber spatula. Give the pans a good bang on the counter to settle the batter evenly into the bottom.

Bake until a toothpick inserted in the middle of each cake comes out clean, about 35 minutes. Let cool on a wire rack for about 30 minutes. Invert the cakes onto wire racks, remove the pans, and let the cakes cool completely.

½ cup sugar

2 tablespoons cornstarch

½ cup cherry juice

2 cups fresh, jarred, or canned
   pitted sour cherries, drained

½ cup kirsch (cherry brandy)

FOR THE CREAM FROSTING:

2 tablespoons unflavored
   powdered gelatin

2 cups milk

½ cup cornstarch

½ cup sugar

4 cups heavy cream, chilled

1 tablespoon vanilla extract

Whole cherries and grated
   chocolate (optional) for garnish

MEANWHILE, MAKE THE CHERRY FILLING: In a small saucepan, whisk together the sugar and cornstarch, then stir in the cherry juice. Bring to a boil and cook until thickened, about 2 minutes. Remove from the heat and pour over the cherries in a heatproof bowl; stir to coat the cherries evenly, then let cool to room temperature. Place one of the cooled cakes on a stand and drizzle it with half of the kirsch. Spread the cherries on top of the cake, then stack the second cake on top; drizzle it with the rest of the kirsch.

MAKE THE CREAM FROSTING: In a small bowl, sprinkle the gelatin over 1 cup of the milk; let sit until the gelatin softens, about 5 minutes. In a medium-size saucepan, whisk the cornstarch and sugar, then add the remaining 1 cup milk. Bring to a boil and cook, stirring constantly, until the mixture thickens to the consistency of very thick pudding. Transfer it to a food processor, along with the gelatin mixture, and process until smooth. Transfer to a large bowl. Put the cream and vanilla in the bowl of a stand mixer fitted with the whisk attachment and beat on medium-high speed until stiff peaks form. Add one third of the whipped cream to the gelatin mixture and whisk until smooth and lightened. Add the remaining whipped cream and gently fold with a rubber spatula until evenly combined.

Spread the frosting evenly over the top and sides of the cake, then refrigerate the cake until the frosting is firm, about 2 hours. Decorate the cake with more cherries and shaved chocolate, if you like.

---

## Good to Know: BAKING SPRAY

When I get ready to bake, I'll admit that the last thing I want to do is butter and flour a pan. I prefer the more modern approach. Baker's Joy is a brand of nonstick cooking spray that coats your pans with a two-in-one mix of fat and flour. Pam also makes a version that works well.

# Bourbon Fruitcake

It's a shame more people don't enjoy fruitcake. When made with fresh-roasted pecans, natural dried fruits, and the best Bourbon or whiskey you can afford, it all adds up to one amazing holiday treat. At Christmastime, I usually polish off half a cake myself. I like to make the cake up to two weeks in advance and age it in Bourbon-soaked cheesecloth, to slightly soften its boozy edge. I promise once you taste this fruitcake, you'll be converting even die-hard fruitcake haters.

---

2 cups drained candied cherries in syrup, such as Amarena Fabbri or other natural candied cherries, halved or roughly chopped

1½ cups packed golden raisins

2 cups Bourbon, such as Maker's Mark or Woodford Reserve, or your favorite whiskey

4 cups pecan halves, toasted and cooled

5 cups cake flour, sifted

2 teaspoons freshly grated nutmeg

1½ teaspoons kosher salt

1 teaspoon baking powder

1½ cups (3 sticks) unsalted butter, softened

2 cups packed dark brown sugar

2 cups granulated sugar

6 large eggs, separated

Two days before you plan to make the cake, combine the cherries, raisins, and Bourbon in a large jar; stir to combine and put the lid on. Let the fruit sit for at least 2 days or up to 1 week to soften in the Bourbon, stirring once a day. Pour into a sieve set over a bowl and reserve the fruit and Bourbon separately.

The day you plan to make the cake, heat the oven to 275°F. Spray a 10-inch Bundt pan evenly with baking spray.

Put the pecans and ½ cup of the flour in a bowl and toss together until evenly coated. Put the remaining 4½ cups flour in another bowl along with the nutmeg, salt, and baking powder and whisk until evenly combined. In the bowl of a stand mixer fitted with the paddle attachment, combine the butter and both sugars and beat together on medium-high speed until lightened, fluffy, and smooth, about 4 minutes, using a rubber spatula to scrape down the side and bottom of the bowl at least once while beating. Add the egg yolks one at a time, beating until smooth before adding the next. With the mixer on low speed, alternately add the dry ingredients and the reserved Bourbon, beginning and ending with the dry ingredients, and mix until just combined and smooth.

Put the egg whites in a large bowl and beat with a whisk or handheld mixer until semistiff peaks form. Add about one third of the whites to the cake batter in the mixer bowl and, using a large rubber spatula, stir to lighten the batter. Add the remaining whites and fold gently until almost incorporated. Add the reserved soaked fruit and the flour-coated pecans and continue folding until all the ingredients are evenly mixed together. Pour into the prepared pan and smooth the top with a rubber spatula. Bang the pan lightly on the counter to settle the batter evenly in the pan. Bake until a toothpick inserted in the middle of the cake between the side and the center tube comes out clean, about 3½ hours. Let cool completely before slicing and serving.

AGE THE FRUITCAKE: If you want to age your cake like I do, soak a 24-inch-square triple layer of cheesecloth in a bowl with 2 cups Bourbon. The cheesecloth should soak most of the Bourbon up, but if not, it's okay. Place two 36-inch-long sheets of aluminum foil on a work surface so they form a plus sign. Gently unfurl the soaked cheesecloth, without squeezing out too much of the Bourbon, in the center of the foil.

Place your cooled fruitcake in the center, and bring the corners and sides of the cheesecloth up and over the fruitcake so it covers the cake completely. If you have any Bourbon left over that didn't soak into the cheesecloth, pour it evenly over the cake now. Bring the sheets of foil up and over the cake so they wrap it completely and snugly. Place the foil-wrapped cake in a large metal tin with a lid and cover it. Let this sit at room temperature or in the refrigerator for 1 week before uncovering, unwrapping, and serving.

# Carrot Sheet Cake

This cake should really be called a chiffon fruitcake because with all the pineapple, coconut, carrots, and nuts included, that's basically what it is—just not super dark and dense like its holiday counterpart. The cream cheese frosting here balances the sweet carrots and coconut and picks up on the tang of the pineapple for a great snack cake that can easily disappear within minutes.

---

FOR THE CAKE:

2 cups all-purpose flour

2 teaspoons baking powder

2 teaspoons baking soda

2 teaspoons ground cinnamon

1 teaspoon kosher salt

1½ cups sugar

¾ cup vegetable or canola oil

½ cup buttermilk

2 teaspoons vanilla extract

4 large eggs

2 cups finely grated carrots

1 cup finely chopped and mashed fresh pineapple

1 cup roughly chopped walnuts or pecans

1 cup unsweetened shredded coconut

½ cup raisins

FOR THE ICING:

1 (8-ounce) package cream cheese, at room temperature

½ cup (1 stick) unsalted butter, at room temperature

½ teaspoon kosher salt

3 cups confectioners' sugar, sifted

1 teaspoon vanilla extract

MAKE THE CAKE: Heat the oven to 350°F. Spray a 9-by-13-inch baking dish evenly with baking spray.

In a large bowl, whisk together the flour, baking powder, baking soda, cinnamon, and salt. In another bowl, whisk together the sugar, oil, buttermilk, vanilla, and eggs. Pour the wet ingredients over the dry ingredients and whisk until evenly combined. Add the carrots, pineapple, walnuts, coconut, and raisins and stir well. Pour the batter into the baking dish, smooth the top with a rubber spatula, then bake until golden brown and a toothpick inserted in the middle of the cake comes out clean, about 45 minutes. Let cool completely, invert the cake onto a wire rack, then invert it again onto a cutting board or serving platter.

MAKE THE ICING: In a large bowl, combine the cream cheese, butter, and salt and, using a handheld mixer, beat until smooth. Add the confectioners' sugar and vanilla and beat on low speed until combined. Increase the speed to high and beat until light and fluffy, about 3 minutes. Spread the frosting evenly over the cake, then cut into squares.

# Cantaloupe Upside-Down Cake

MAKES ONE 12-INCH CAKE

In the South, we love melon but sometimes despair of what to do with summer's bumper crop of cantaloupe, besides another giant fruit salad or delicate sorbet. Cantaloupe is so mild in flavor that it pairs best with a plain butter cake. The key to keeping your design beautiful and in place while pouring the batter over the slices is to let the butter and sugar in the bottom of the pan cool with the fruit slices until firm, then pour the batter gently so as not to push the fruit around. That way, you'll have a gorgeous cake once it's turned over.

20 tablespoons (2½ sticks) unsalted butter

3 teaspoons vanilla extract

10 tablespoons packed light brown sugar

2 tablespoons rum

12 slices peeled cantaloupe

1¾ cups all-purpose flour

1 tablespoon baking powder

½ teaspoon kosher salt

1 cup granulated sugar

3 large eggs

⅓ cup buttermilk

Melt 8 tablespoons (1 stick) of the butter in a 12-inch nonstick or cast-iron skillet over medium-high heat. Whisk in 1 teaspoon of the vanilla, the brown sugar, and rum until the sugar is dissolved. Remove from the heat and arrange 8 cantaloupe slices in a starburst pattern across the bottom of the skillet; halve the remaining slices crosswise and use them to fill in gaps between the slices. Let the skillet cool completely to room temperature so the butter mixture solidifies, anchoring the cantaloupe slices.

Heat the oven to 350°F.

In a bowl, combine the flour, baking powder, and salt. In another bowl, beat together the remaining 12 tablespoons butter (1½ sticks), the remaining 2 teaspoons vanilla, and the granulated sugar with a handheld mixer until pale and fluffy, at least 4 minutes. Add the eggs one at a time, beating well after each. Alternately add the dry ingredients and buttermilk and continue beating until smooth. Pour the batter over the slices in the skillet and smooth the top with a rubber spatula. Bake until the cake is golden brown and a toothpick inserted in the middle comes out clean, about 35 minutes. Let cool in the skillet for 10 minutes, then carefully invert onto a wire rack and let cool completely.

# Caramel Cake

MAKES ONE 9-INCH LAYER CAKE

This is a cake straight out of my dreams. Dense yellow butter cake sandwiched and slathered with a solid caramel fudge icing. Sometimes it looks as straight as an arrow, sometimes it's slumped and ugly, beautiful in the way a truffle prides itself on its bumps and lumps. But the taste is always exquisite and lingers in your memory long after the cake is eaten. It's my favorite lesson on not judging a book by its cover.

Caramel cake can be a little challenging to execute the first time because of the beaten fudge icing, which has to be just the right consistency to be spread—not too runny or too stiff. Only practice will get you comfortable enough with the icing to truly know when and how to spread it. Luckily, this cake is supposed to be an ugly duckling.

---

FOR THE CAKE:

3 cups cake flour, sifted

2½ teaspoons baking powder

1 teaspoon kosher salt

1 cup whole milk

2 teaspoons vanilla extract

1 cup (2 sticks) unsalted butter, at room temperature

1½ cups sugar

4 large eggs

FOR THE ICING:

3½ cups sugar

¾ cup (1½ sticks) unsalted butter, melted

2 (15-ounce) cans evaporated milk

¼ cup homemade "corn syrup" (page 90)

1 large egg

2 teaspoons vanilla extract

1 teaspoon baking soda

MAKE THE CAKE: Heat the oven to 350°F. Spray three 9-inch round cake pans evenly with baking spray.

In a large bowl, combine the flour, baking powder, and salt. In a glass measuring cup, combine the milk and vanilla. In the bowl of a stand mixer fitted with the paddle attachment, combine the butter and sugar and beat until pale and fluffy, about 3 minutes. Add the eggs one at a time, beating well after each, until the batter is smooth. Turn the mixer speed to low and alternately add the dry ingredients and the milk mixture, beginning and ending with the dry ingredients; beat until just combined and smooth. Divide the batter evenly among the cake pans and smooth the tops. Give the pans a good bang on the counter to settle the batter evenly in the bottom. Bake, rotating the pans halfway through baking, until lightly browned at the edges and a toothpick inserted in the middle comes out clean, about 25 minutes. Let cool in the pans on wire racks for 25 minutes, then invert and remove the pans. Let cakes cool completely.

MAKE THE ICING: Combine 3 cups of the sugar, the butter, evaporated milk, corn syrup, and egg in a 6-quart copper saucepan or Dutch oven. Put the remaining ½ cup sugar in a small skillet and cook over high heat, swirling the skillet constantly, until the sugar melts into an amber-colored liquid caramel, about 2 minutes. Pour the caramel into the copper saucepan, attach a candy thermometer to the side, and cook over medium heat, stirring constantly on the bottom with a wooden spoon to prevent scorching, until the thermometer reaches 234°F, 40 to 45 minutes. Remove from the heat and immediately add the vanilla and baking soda; stir until smooth, then let sit for 1 minute. Using a handheld mixer, beat the caramel on medium speed until it reaches the consistency of loose pudding, 1 to 2 minutes.

Working quickly, place one layer on a cake stand and evenly pour about ½ cup of the caramel icing over the surface of the cake (eyeball this amount; it doesn't need to be exact, and using a measuring cup will only slow you down). Place the second layer on top and evenly pour about another ½ cup of the caramel icing over the surface of the cake. Place the third layer on top and steadily

and evenly pour the remaining caramel icing over the cake, trying to evenly disperse it while pouring. Using an offset spatula, quickly spread the icing falling over the sides of the cake over the other layers until it covers the sides completely. Let the icing cool completely to set the icing before serving. Store any remaining cake at room temperature, covered in a cake dome or loosely wrapped in plastic wrap, for up to 5 days.

TIP: Using a copper pot and a reliable candy thermometer will go a long way toward helping you make the icing for this cake. A new thermometer will guarantee accurate temperature results so your icing isn't over- or undercooked. Copper retains heat longer than steel, which means when you begin icing the cake the icing that remains in the pan will stay soft enough to still be poured on at the end. If using a regular aluminum or steel pot, the contents can cool off too quickly, thus leaving you with set fudge that refuses to be spread onto the cake. A rotating cake stand and small offset spatula will also help you get the icing on quickly and efficiently, lessening the risk of it setting before you have the icing completely on the cake.

# Cinnamon-Chocolate Spekkuk

MAKES ONE 8-INCH SQUARE CAKE

When I first started working at *Saveur*, my boss, James Oseland, implored me to make this cake over and over, his favorite from his time living and eating in Southeast Asia. *Spekkuk* is an Indonesian cake based on baking traditions introduced by Dutch colonists. Its distinctive stripes are made by baking thin layers of batter—here, one cinnamon and one chocolate—on top of one another. This cake will take about 2 hours of baking time. Although it seems like the first layer would be burnt by the time the last layer is baked through, I assure you it won't be. The subsequent layers insulate the first ones and with all the breaks from heat going in and out of the oven, it never gets a chance to burn. The edges will be slightly dry and crisp, but that's a boon here, lending it a cookie-like texture at the edges. The high egg content gives the cake a dense, moist interior—a perfect foil for coffee in the afternoon.

---

3 cups cake flour, sifted

4½ teaspoons ground cinnamon

2 teaspoons freshly grated nutmeg

¾ teaspoon baking powder

¼ teaspoon ground cloves

1 teaspoon kosher salt

2¼ cups (4½ sticks) unsalted butter, softened

2½ cups sugar

6 large eggs

4 large egg yolks, lightly beaten

1 tablespoon vanilla extract

3 ounces dark chocolate, melted

3 tablespoons Dutch-process cocoa powder

Heat the oven to 325°F. Spray an 8-inch square baking pan evenly with baking spray.

In a bowl, whisk together the flour, cinnamon, nutmeg, baking powder, cloves, and salt. In the bowl of a stand mixer fitted with the paddle attachment, combine the butter and sugar and beat on medium-high speed until pale and fluffy, about 4 minutes. Add the eggs one at a time, beating well after each, then beat in the egg yolks and vanilla. Add the dry ingredients and beat until just combined. Divide the batter in half and stir the melted chocolate and cocoa powder into one half until smooth.

Pour one quarter of the chocolate batter into the prepared pan, spreading it evenly over the bottom, and bake until it springs back when lightly touched, about 14 minutes. Remove from the oven and carefully pour one quarter of the plain batter over the cake; repeat the baking process. Repeat the pouring and baking process with the remaining batters, using a quarter of each at a time, until all the batter is used and the cake is done.

Let cool completely. Run a knife carefully around the edges of the pan to loosen the cake, then invert it onto a cutting board. Invert again and cut into large squares.

# Coconut Cake

MAKES ONE 9-INCH LAYER CAKE

I can't imagine a cake I like more than this one. Saturated with fragrant coconut water, this cake will never dry out, and both its flavor and texture actually improve the longer it sits or "ages," up to 3 days. Using a fresh coconut and coconut water makes all the difference for this cake. You can make it with packaged ingredients, but you'll be missing that bright, unadulterated coconut flavor, and once you try it you'll see how worth the effort it really is.

---

FOR THE CAKE:

2½ cups cake flour, sifted

1 teaspoon baking soda

1 teaspoon kosher salt

1 cup buttermilk

1 tablespoon vanilla extract

1 cup (2 sticks) unsalted butter, softened

2 cups sugar

5 large eggs

FOR THE FROSTING:

4 large egg whites

½ teaspoon cream of tartar

2¼ cups sugar

¼ cup homemade "corn syrup" (page 90)

1 teaspoon kosher salt

2 teaspoons vanilla extract

¾ cup fresh coconut water

3 cups freshly grated coconut (see page 26)

MAKE THE CAKE: Heat the oven to 350°F. Spray two 9-inch round cake pans evenly with baking spray.

In a bowl, whisk together the flour, baking soda, and salt. In a glass measuring cup, whisk together the buttermilk and vanilla. In the bowl of a stand mixer fitted with the paddle attachment, combine the butter and sugar and beat on medium-high speed until pale and fluffy, about 3 minutes. Add the eggs one at a time, beating well after each. On low speed, alternately add the dry ingredients and buttermilk and beat until smooth. Divide the batter between the prepared pans and smooth the top. Lightly knock the pans on the counter to settle the batter into the pans. Bake until a toothpick inserted in the middle comes out clean, about 35 minutes. Let cool in the pans for 20 minutes, then invert onto wire racks and let cool completely. Using a serrated knife, split each cake horizontally, producing four layers.

MAKE THE FROSTING: Put the egg whites and cream of tartar in the bowl of a stand mixer fitted with the whisk attachment and whisk on medium-high speed until soft peaks form; turn the mixer off. In a small saucepan, bring the sugar, ½ cup water, the syrup, and salt to a boil over high heat, stirring to dissolve the sugar. Attach a candy thermometer to the side of the pan and continue cooking, without stirring, until the thermometer reads 250°F, 4 to 5 minutes. Turn the stand mixer to medium speed and very slowly

drizzle the hot syrup into the beating egg whites, trying your best to avoid letting the syrup hit the beaters or the side of the bowl. Add the vanilla, increase the speed to high, and whisk until the meringue triples in volume, forms stiff peaks, and is slightly warm to the touch, about 3 minutes.

Place one cake layer on a stand, drizzle evenly with 3 tablespoons of the coconut water, spread with about 1½ cups frosting, then sprinkle with ½ cup of the grated coconut; repeat this layering until you reach the last layer of cake, then drizzle it with the remaining coconut water. Cover the top and sides of the stacked cakes with the remaining frosting, then use your hands to gently press the remaining coconut all over the cake so that it adheres. Refrigerate the cake to firm the frosting before serving.

## Good to Know: COCONUT GRATING

When I first discovered the coconut rotary graters used in India to shred fresh coconut for use in making coconut milk and confections, my life changed. The grater produces the perfect-size shavings for my Coconut Cake, yielding fluffy piles instead of heavier, long shreds. It makes shredding coconut a much easier task and really fun. Simply split a coconut in half, press each half against the rotating ball grater, and turn the handle to get quick, fine shreds. It attaches to virtually any surface via a sturdy suction cup at its base. The model I use and cherish was brought back from India by a coworker, but these graters are also available online (check Amazon or eBay), and possibly at your local ethnic grocery or market.

If you don't want to purchase a special tool for grating coconut, the food processor is the next best thing, and it'll produce similar results. You can buy whole coconuts, crack them open, and pry out the meat yourself, or purchase whole chunks of coconut from your grocery store. Once you have the cleaned white coconut pieces, simply toss them into the bowl of a food processor fitted with its normal blade (not the shredding disk). Pulse the processor for about 10 seconds, and you should have finely ground, light shreds of coconut, ready to use in your coconut cake, or for toasting and sprinkling over Marbled Chocolate Bark (page 187), or to add to your bowl of granola for breakfast.

# Cinnamon Crumb Cake

MAKES ONE 8-INCH SQUARE CAKE

I remember venturing out to Seneca Avenue in Queens, when I first moved to New York City, to visit Rudy's Pastry Shop, a well-known and beloved German bakery that was renowned for its crumb cakes. I'd had crumb cakes before, but none with such a glorious layer of crumb on top; it was a revelation. Since then I've been unable to make a crumb cake without that substantial crumb topping, which is basically made up of balls of shortbread dough, baked to crunchy, buttery perfection. What's not to love?

1 cup (2 sticks) unsalted butter, melted

1¼ cups granulated sugar

6 tablespoons packed light brown sugar

2 tablespoons ground cinnamon

1¼ teaspoons kosher salt

3¾ cups all-purpose flour, plus more for the pan

2½ teaspoons baking powder

1 cup milk

6 tablespoons sour cream

2¼ teaspoons vanilla extract

2 large eggs

Heat the oven to 325°F. Spray an 8-inch square baking pan evenly with baking spray.

In a medium-size bowl, combine ½ cup of the butter, ¼ cup of the granulated sugar, the brown sugar, 1 tablespoon of the cinnamon, and ½ teaspoon of the salt in a bowl and stir until smooth. Add 1½ cups of the flour and stir with a fork until crumbly; refrigerate the crumb topping until ready to use.

In a large bowl, whisk together the remaining 2¼ cups flour, 1 cup sugar, ¾ teaspoon salt, and the baking powder. In a large measuring cup, whisk together the remaining ½ cup butter, the milk, sour cream, vanilla, and eggs until smooth. Pour the wet ingredients over the dry ingredients and whisk to combine. Pour the batter into the prepared pan and sprinkle the chilled crumble topping over the top. (Don't worry, it will seem like an inordinate amount of crumble for the batter, but it's supposed to be that way, and trust me: You will love the results.) Bake until a toothpick inserted in the middle of the cake comes out clean, about 1 hour 15 minutes. Let cool completely before cutting into squares.

TIP: This is a basic recipe. Feel free to swap the cinnamon out for ground cardamom, ground ginger, or freshly grated nutmeg. Stir about 1 cup chopped chocolate into the batter too, if you like.

# Coconut-Lime Cornmeal Pound Cake

MAKES ONE 9-BY-5-INCH LOAF CAKE

The chef at a café in Starkville, Mississippi, where I worked after college, wanted me to come up with some kind of bread to serve with her curried chicken salad. Back then, curry meant the tropics to me, so I used a basic pound cake recipe, used half cornmeal and half flour, threw in some lime zest and sweetened shredded coconut, and this gem popped out of the oven. Because it's not too sweet, this cake still makes a great accompaniment to a lunch that straddles the sweet-savory line.

FOR THE CAKE:

1 cup all-purpose flour

1 cup yellow cornmeal

1 tablespoon baking powder

1 teaspoon kosher salt

½ cup unsweetened coconut milk

Grated zest of 1 lime

2 tablespoons fresh lime juice

1 teaspoon vanilla extract

½ cup (1 stick) unsalted butter, at cool room temperature

¾ cup granulated sugar

4 large eggs, at room temperature

½ cup freshly grated or packaged shredded coconut

FOR THE GLAZE:

2 cups confectioners' sugar

2 tablespoons unsweetened coconut milk

Grated zest of 1 lime

MAKE THE CAKE: Heat the oven to 350°F. Spray an 8- or 9-by-5-inch loaf pan evenly with baking spray.

In a bowl, whisk together the flour, cornmeal, baking powder, and salt. In a glass measuring cup, whisk together the coconut milk, lime zest, vanilla, and lime juice. In the bowl of a stand mixer fitted with the paddle attachment, combine the butter and sugar and beat on medium-high speed until pale and fluffy, about 3 minutes. Add the eggs one at a time, beating well after each. On low speed, alternately add the dry ingredients and the coconut milk mixture and beat until smooth. Stir in the coconut, then pour the batter into the prepared pan and smooth the top. Lightly knock the pan on the counter to settle the batter into the pan. Bake until a toothpick inserted in the middle comes out clean, about 45 minutes. Let cool in the pan for 20 minutes, then invert onto a wire rack and let cool completely.

MAKE THE GLAZE: Whisk together the confectioners' sugar, coconut milk, and lime zest in a bowl, then drizzle it over the cooled cake. Let sit for about 10 minutes to set the glaze.

# Coffee Tres Leches

MAKES ONE 9-BY-13-INCH CAKE

I've always loved tres leches cake. Saturated to the point of almost being pudding, it is still cake: This idea is enthralling to me. As a point of reference, consider tiramisù, in which ladyfingers (essentially cake) are soaked in boozy sweet espresso and layered with eggy sabayon and whipped cream.

In this recipe, I incorporate the aspect of tiramisù I love most—the coffee—so you can get your caffeine fix along with your chilled milky dessert. It's like a blended coffee drink and cake in one. And I have to admit, it's my new favorite.

---

2 cups all-purpose flour

¼ cup Dutch-process cocoa powder

4 teaspoons baking powder

1 teaspoon kosher salt

6 large eggs, separated, at room temperature

1½ cups sugar

½ cup milk

1 cup heavy cream, plus more cream, whipped and lightly sweetened, for serving

1 (14-ounce) can sweetened condensed milk

1 (12-ounce) can evaporated milk

½ cup brewed espresso, cooled

Heat the oven to 325°F. Spray a 9-by-13-inch baking pan evenly with baking spray.

In a bowl, whisk together the flour, cocoa powder, baking powder, and salt. Put the egg whites in the bowl of a stand mixer fitted with the whisk attachment and beat on medium speed until soft peaks begin to form. Gradually add the sugar while mixing, then increase the speed to high and beat until stiff peaks form. Whisk in the egg yolks, then the milk, then remove the bowl from the mixer and gently fold in the dry ingredients until evenly incorporated and no pockets of flour remain. Pour into the prepared pan, smooth the top with a rubber spatula, and bake until a toothpick inserted in the middle comes out clean, 30 to 35 minutes. Let cool completely.

In a pitcher, whisk together the 1 cup cream, the sweetened condensed milk, evaporated milk, and espresso, then slowly drizzle the mixture over the cake until all of it is used (don't worry, the cake may look like it's drowning in too much liquid, but it will absorb it eventually). Wrap the cake in plastic and refrigerate until it absorbs all the cream, at least 2 hours or up to overnight. Cut into squares and serve chilled with a large dollop of whipped cream on top.

# Cream Cheese Pound Cake

MAKES ONE 10-INCH TUBE OR BUNDT CAKE

Talk about an indulgence! This is not your ordinary everyday pound cake. This cake has creamy depth and—oh, my god!—a perfect, super-crunchy crust that everyone fights over because of how addictive and amazing it is. The low oven temperature keeps the cake dense and moist, and a good couple days of aging wrapped tightly in plastic wrap at room temperature does wonders for its flavor and texture, while retaining that crunchy crust. I've been known to toast a slice in the morning and slather it with butter for breakfast.

1½ cups (3 sticks) unsalted butter,
    at room temperature

1 (8-ounce) package cream cheese,
    at room temperature

3 cups sugar

2 teaspoons vanilla extract

1 teaspoon kosher salt

6 large eggs

3 cups cake flour

Heat the oven to 275°F. Spray a 10-inch tube or Bundt cake pan evenly with baking spray.

Put the butter and cream cheese in the bowl of a stand mixer fitted with the paddle attachment. Beat on medium-high speed until smooth. Add the sugar, vanilla, and salt and beat again until the mixture is fluffy and smooth, about 5 minutes. Add the eggs one at a time, beating after each until the mixture is completely incorporated and smooth. Add the flour and beat on low speed until the flour is just absorbed and the batter is smooth. Pour the batter into the prepared pan and smooth the top with a rubber spatula. Give the pan a good bang on the counter to settle the batter evenly into the pan. Bake until the cake develops a crusty, golden brown matte top and a toothpick inserted halfway between the edge and center hole comes out clean, about 1½ hours. Let cool in the pan on a wire rack for about 30 minutes, then invert the cake onto the wire rack, remove the pan, and let the cake cool completely before serving.

You can wrap the cooled cake in plastic wrap and it will get better the longer it sits, or "ages," so make it a couple days ahead if you have the time.

# German Chocolate Cupcakes

MAKES 12 CUPCAKES

I find that German chocolate cake is best made as cupcakes: literal cake cups to hold all the luscious, loose coconut-pecan filling that always steals the spotlight from the cake anyway. This is a treat that encourages you to have fun with your food, turning and twisting the cupcake in your hands to keep gravity from taking the precious filling away from you.

FOR THE ICING:

½ cup sugar

2 large egg yolks

¾ cup evaporated milk

6 tablespoons (¾ stick) unsalted butter, melted

½ teaspoon kosher salt

1 cup pecans, toasted and roughly chopped

1 cup lightly packed sweetened shredded coconut

1 teaspoon vanilla extract

FOR THE CUPCAKES:

2 ounces German's sweet chocolate, finely chopped

3 tablespoons boiling water

¼ cup all-purpose flour

¼ cup pecans, toasted and roughly chopped

1 cup confectioners' sugar, sifted

½ teaspoon kosher salt

5 tablespoons unsalted butter, melted

1 teaspoon vanilla extract

2 large egg whites, at room temperature

MAKE THE ICING: In a small saucepan, whisk together the sugar and egg yolks until smooth. Stir in the evaporated milk, butter, and salt, then heat over medium heat, stirring occasionally. When the mixture begins to simmer, continue stirring steadily until it thickens slightly and coats the back of a spoon, about 2 minutes. Remove from the heat and stir in the pecans, coconut, and vanilla. Transfer to a bowl and let cool completely to room temperature. Refrigerate until ready to use.

MAKE THE CUPCAKES: Heat the oven to 350°F. Spray a 12-cup muffin tin evenly with baking spray.

Put the chocolate in a small bowl and pour the boiling water over it. Cover the bowl with a small piece of plastic wrap to seal in the heat and let sit for 1 minute. Uncover and stir with a spoon until the chocolate is smooth.

Meanwhile, put the flour and pecans in a food processor and process until finely ground. Add the confectioners' sugar and salt and process until very finely ground (make sure you scrape the side of the bowl once or twice with a rubber spatula to make sure everything's mixed together evenly). Add the butter, vanilla, and egg whites and process briefly until the batter just comes together and is smooth. Divide the batter evenly among the muffin cups and smooth the tops with a rubber spatula. Bake until a toothpick inserted in each comes out clean, about 25 minutes. Let cool for 5 minutes, then invert the cupcakes onto a wire rack and let cool completely.

The edges of the cupcakes should be raised above their middles. If the middles also have a small raised hump, scoop it away with a spoon to level it off. When ready to serve, spoon some of the icing on top of each cupcake, letting it settle into the "cup" on top of the cake.

# Hummingbird Cake

This classic, over-the-top cake first garnered fame in *Southern Living* magazine in the 1970s and has been a staple of southern potlucks ever since. Bananas and pineapple are baked into a spiced yellow cake, which is bathed in a rich cream cheese icing. Its slightly tropical, down-home appeal makes it an ideal dessert for picnics or warm summer days when even the heat can't keep your cake craving at bay.

FOR THE CAKE:

3 cups all-purpose flour, plus more for dusting

2 teaspoons ground cinnamon

1 teaspoon baking soda

1 teaspoon salt

1 cup finely chopped pecans

1½ cups granulated sugar

1 cup packed light brown sugar

3 large eggs, beaten

1 (8-ounce) can crushed pineapple, juice reserved, or 1 cup pureed fresh pineapple

2 cups mashed ripe bananas (about 5 bananas)

1 cup canola oil

2 teaspoons vanilla extract

FOR THE FROSTING:

¾ cup (1½ sticks) unsalted butter, at room temperature

2 (8-ounce) packages cream cheese, at room temperature

1 tablespoon vanilla extract

2 cups confectioners' sugar, sifted

Chopped pecans for garnish

MAKE THE CAKE: Heat the oven to 350°F. Spray three 9-inch round cake pans evenly with baking spray.

In a bowl, combine the flour, cinnamon, baking soda, and salt; stir in the pecans. In a large bowl, combine the granulated sugar, brown sugar, and eggs and whisk until smooth. Add the pineapple and juice, bananas, oil, and vanilla and whisk until the batter is smooth. Add the dry ingredients and whisk until just combined and smooth. Divide the batter evenly among the prepared pans and smooth the tops. Give the pans a good bang on the counter to settle the batter evenly into the bottom of the pans. Bake, rotating the pans halfway through baking, until a toothpick inserted in the middle comes out clean, about 40 minutes. Let cool in the pans for 25 minutes, then invert the cakes onto wire racks and let cool completely. (The cakes can be wrapped in plastic and set aside for up to 1 day.)

MAKE THE FROSTING: In a bowl, combine the butter and cream cheese and beat with a handheld mixer until smooth. Add the vanilla and confectioners' sugar and beat on high speed until light and fluffy. Place a cake layer on a cake stand and, using a small ubber or offset spatula, spread 1 cup of the frosting evenly over the top. Place the second cake layer on top and frost with another cup of frosting. Repeat with the remaining cake layer, then spread the remaining frosting over the top and sides of the cake. Sprinkle with the chopped pecans and refrigerate to firm the frosting, at least 1 hour. Serve chilled or at room temperature.

# Lemon Layer Cake

What a stunner! This cake is quite possibly the best vehicle for lemon I know. Lemon zest is baked into the cake, then the cake is doused in tart lemon syrup and sandwiched with a very lemony buttercream frosting. I love it as an afternoon snack in the doldrums of winter, a bright spark in a dreary day. To gild the lily, enjoy it with a glass of lemonade.

FOR THE CAKE:

2½ cups cake flour, sifted

2½ teaspoons baking powder

1 teaspoon kosher salt

½ cup milk

1 teaspoon vanilla extract

1 cup (2 sticks) unsalted butter, softened

1½ cups sugar

1 tablespoon grated lemon zest

4 large eggs

FOR THE SYRUP:

¼ cup sugar

⅓ cup fresh lemon juice

FOR THE FROSTING:

1½ cups sugar

¼ cup cornstarch

¼ cup grated lemon zest

1 teaspoon kosher salt

10 large egg yolks

1 cup fresh lemon juice

1½ cups (3 sticks) unsalted butter, softened

1 teaspoon vanilla extract

MAKE THE CAKE: Heat the oven to 350°F. Spray three 9-inch round cake pans evenly with baking spray.

In a bowl, whisk together the flour, baking powder, and salt. In another bowl, whisk together the milk and vanilla. In the bowl of a stand mixer fitted with the paddle attachment, beat the butter, sugar, and lemon zest on medium-high speed until pale and fluffy, about 3 minutes. Add the eggs one at a time, beating well after each. On low speed, alternately add the dry ingredients and the milk mixture. Divide the batter among the prepared pans and smooth the tops with a rubber spatula. Knock the pans lightly on the counter to settle the batter evenly in the pans. Bake until a toothpick inserted in the middle comes out clean, about 30 minutes. Let cool in the pans for 20 minutes, then invert onto wire racks and let cool completely.

MAKE THE SYRUP: In a small saucepan, bring the sugar and lemon juice to a boil over high heat. Remove from the heat and set aside.

MAKE THE FROSTING: In a medium-size saucepan, whisk together the sugar, cornstarch, lemon zest, and salt. Add the egg yolks and whisk until smooth, then stir in the juice. Stirring often, bring to a boil over medium heat and cook, stirring constantly, until very thick, about 3 minutes. Remove from the heat and transfer to a bowl. Cover with plastic wrap and refrigerate the lemon curd until thick and cold.

In the bowl of a stand mixer fitted with the paddle attachment, beat the butter and one quarter of the chilled curd on medium-high speed until fluffy and smooth, about 1 minute. Add half of the remaining curd, beating until smooth, then add the remaining curd and the vanilla. Increase the speed to high and beat the frosting until pale and fluffy, about 3 minutes.

Place one cake layer on a cake stand, drizzle with 3 tablespoons of the syrup, and spread with 1 cup frosting. Top with another cake, drizzle with 3 tablespoons of the syrup, and spread with 1 cup frosting. Top with the remaining cake and drizzle with the remaining syrup. Cover the top and sides with the remaining frosting; chill the cake to firm the frosting, at least 1 hour. Let come to room temperature before serving.

# Lemon-Lime Soda Cake

Soda is a popular ingredient in cakes in the South, in part because it adds sweetness and lightness from the carbonation, and because of the kitschy tradition (Coke is made in Atlanta, after all). I've had many a cake made with Coke or Dr Pepper, and, while novel, they end up tasting nothing like the sodas themselves. However, using a tart citrus soda, especially an all-natural variety like Boylan, brightens a relatively plain yellow cake, and the glaze, incorporating more of the soda, enhances the refreshing taste further. It's pure silly fun, but often that's just what cake is for.

FOR THE CAKE:

2½ cups all-purpose flour

2½ teaspoons baking powder

1 teaspoon kosher salt

1 cup lemon-lime soda,
    such as Boylan or 7-Up

Grated zest of 1 lemon

Grated zest of 1 lime

1 cup (2 sticks) unsalted butter,
    softened

1½ cups sugar

4 large eggs

FOR THE GLAZE:

2 cups confectioners' sugar

¼ cup lemon-lime soda,
    such as Boylan or 7-Up

Grated zest of 1 lemon

MAKE THE CAKE: Heat the oven to 350°F. Spray a 9-by-13-inch baking pan evenly with baking spray.

In a bowl, whisk together the flour, baking powder, and salt. In another bowl, whisk together the soda and lemon and lime zests. In a third bowl, combine the butter and sugar and, using a handheld mixer, beat on high speed until fluffy. Add the eggs one at a time, beating well after each until the batter is smooth. Alternately add the dry ingredients and the soda mixture, beating until smooth. Pour the batter into the prepared pan, smoothing the top. Bake, rotating halfway through, until a toothpick inserted in the middle comes out clean, about 30 minutes. Let cool completely.

MAKE THE GLAZE: In a bowl, combine the confectioners' sugar, soda, and lemon zest and whisk until smooth. Pour the glaze evenly over the cake and let sit to harden before serving.

# Marbled Orange-Chocolate Bundt Cake

MAKES ONE 10-INCH BUNDT CAKE

There are few things more impressive than a marbled cake. The fact that it's the type of aesthetic artistry that any novice can pull off makes it all the more appealing. As my favorite cookbook author, Nigella Lawson, said in *How to Be a Domestic Goddess*, the book that's influenced my cooking more than any other, "Everyone seems to think it's hard to make a cake . . . no need to disillusion them."

This cake is based on one that my friend and mentor Nick Malgieri taught me to make years ago, from Demel, the famed pastry shop in Vienna, Austria. I incorporate orange zest and juice into the cake batter, and marble the batter with milk chocolate. It's a simple stunner of a cake, best served in generous wedges with tea in the afternoon.

4 ounces milk chocolate, roughly chopped

¼ cup Grand Marnier or other orange liqueur

3 cups all-purpose flour

6 tablespoons cornstarch

1 teaspoon kosher salt

2 cups (4 sticks) unsalted butter, softened

2½ cups sugar

Grated zest of 2 oranges

1 tablespoon vanilla extract

10 large eggs, separated

Heat the oven to 325°F. Spray a 10-inch metal Bundt pan evenly with baking spray.

Set a medium-size heatproof bowl over a small saucepan of simmering water and add the chocolate to the bowl (make sure the bowl does not touch the water). Stir until melted, then remove from the heat and stir in the liqueur until smooth. In a bowl, whisk together the flour, cornstarch, and salt. In a separate bowl, combine the butter, ½ cup of the sugar, the orange zest, and vanilla and beat with a handheld mixer on medium speed until pale and fluffy, about 2 minutes. Add the egg yolks one at a time, beating well after each until smooth. Add the dry ingredients and beat until just combined.

In a large bowl, beat the egg whites with a handheld mixer on high speed until frothy. Sprinkle in the remaining 2 cups sugar and beat until stiff peaks form. Whisk one third of the egg whites into the cake batter to lighten it, then, using a rubber spatula, gently fold in the remaining egg whites.

Fold one third of the cake batter into the chocolate. Pour half of the remaining plain cake batter into the prepared Bundt pan and smooth the top. Pour all the chocolate batter into the pan, top with the remaining plain batter, and smooth the top with a rubber spatula. Using a butter knife, swirl the chocolate batter into the cake batter to create a marbled effect. Smooth the top once more, then bake until a toothpick inserted halfway between the outside edge and center hole the comes out clean, about 55 minutes. Let cool in the pan for 20 minutes, then invert the cake onto a wire rack and let cool completely.

# Mississippi Mud Cake

MAKES ONE 9-BY-13-INCH CAKE

This treat, named for the thick, dense clay mud in Mississippi, is a chocolate lover's dream. Somewhere between a pie and a cake, Mississippi mud is a brownie-like layer of chocolate with a fluffy white marshmallow top, the whole thing covered in fudge sauce: It's the love child of a Mallomar and rocky road ice cream. In my update, a rich chocolate and espresso cake is topped with homemade marshmallow icing mixed with toasted pecans and covered in a caramel fudge sauce. It's a guilty pleasure you can wallow in without shame.

FOR THE CAKE:

2½ cups all-purpose flour

¼ cup Dutch-process cocoa powder

1 teaspoon baking soda

1 teaspoon kosher salt

½ cup boiling water

8 ounces dark chocolate, finely chopped

2 cups sugar

1 cup (2 sticks) unsalted butter

1 teaspoon vanilla extract

4 large eggs

1 cup buttermilk

FOR THE MARSHMALLOW TOPPING:

1 cup sugar

4 large egg whites

1 teaspoon cornstarch

½ teaspoon cream of tartar

2 cups pecan halves

MAKE THE CAKE: Heat the oven to 350°F. Spray a 9-by-13-inch baking pan evenly with baking spray.

In a bowl, whisk together the flour, cocoa powder, baking soda, and salt. Put the chocolate in a heatproof bowl and pour the boiling water over it; let sit for 1 minute to melt the chocolate, then stir until smooth. In the bowl of a stand mixer fitted with the paddle attachment, combine the sugar, butter, and vanilla and beat on medium-high speed until fluffy, about 3 minutes. Add the eggs one at a time, beating well after each until the batter is smooth. Stir the buttermilk into the chocolate and alternately add it to the batter with the dry ingredients. Pour the batter into the prepared pan, smooth the top, and bake, rotating halfway through, until a toothpick inserted in the middle comes out clean, about 40 minutes. Let cool completely.

MAKE THE MARSHMALLOW TOPPING: Put the sugar and ½ cup water in a small saucepan and bring to a boil with a candy thermometer attached to the side of the pan. Put the egg whites, cornstarch, and cream of tartar in the bowl of a stand mixer fitted with the whisk attachment and beat on medium speed until soft peaks form. Cook the syrup until it reaches 240°F on the thermometer, then slowly drizzle it into the beating egg whites. Continue beating until glossy, stiff peaks form and the meringue is just warm to the touch.

1 cup sugar

½ cup heavy cream, at room
temperature

4 tablespoons (½ stick) unsalted
butter, at room temperature

2 ounces dark chocolate, finely
chopped

2 tablespoons whiskey or Bourbon

Flaky sea salt

Stir in the pecans, then cover the cake with the meringue, creating swirls and peaks with a rubber spatula. Use a blowtorch to brown the top (see below), then let cool while you make the caramel fudge sauce.

MAKE THE CARAMEL FUDGE SAUCE: Put the sugar in a small saucepan and cook over medium-high heat, swirling the pan constantly, until the sugar turns to liquid caramel and no solid sugar remains. Remove from the heat and add the cream and butter; stir until smooth, returning to medium heat, if necessary, to re-melt any seized caramel. Add the chocolate, let sit for 1 minute, then stir again until smooth. Stir in the whiskey, then drizzle over the cake. Sprinkle with sea salt before serving each portion with more sauce on the side.

## Good to Know: HOW TO USE A HANDHELD TORCH

Many of my recipes, such as the Lemon Meringue Pie (page 84), Buttermilk Île Flottante (page 145), and Mint Julep Crème Brûlée (page 151), call for using a handheld torch to brown their meringues. Old southern recipes always called for browning meringues in a broiler. And while this will achieve the end goal, using a handheld blowtorch achieves a more attractive and even result. The blowtorches might seem intimidating, but I assure you they're as easy as using a handheld lighter. The key is a steady hand: Instead of waving the flame quickly back and forth over the meringue, hold the flame steadily on one spot and slowly move it over the meringue as it browns, which will take 1 or 2 seconds per spot. My favorite model is the C.R. Laurence propane torch, available online and in hardware stores, but if you prefer a smaller, more stylish torch, I like the 6½-inch Messermeister Cheflamme culinary torch, available online or at your local kitchenwares store.

# Raspberry and Apple Coffee Cake

MAKES ONE 9-INCH CAKE

A lot of fruit-filled cakes usually incorporate fruit in a puree or on the top, but I love this cake because it's chock-full of crisp apple and raspberries, with barely enough batter to hold it together. The excess moisture from the fruit keeps it soft and tender throughout the long baking time.

2½ cups all-purpose flour

2¼ teaspoons baking powder

1 teaspoon ground cinnamon

1 teaspoon kosher salt

¾ cup buttermilk

1½ teaspoons vanilla extract

Grated zest of 1 orange

¾ cup (1½ sticks) unsalted butter, softened

1 cup sugar

4 large eggs

2 tart green apples, cored, peeled, and finely chopped

12 ounces raspberries

Whipped cream for garnish

Heat the oven to 350°F. Spray a 9-inch springform pan evenly with baking spray.

In a bowl, whisk together the flour, baking powder, cinnamon, and salt. In another bowl, whisk together the buttermilk, vanilla, and orange zest. In a third bowl, combine the butter and sugar and beat with a handheld mixer on medium-high speed until pale and fluffy, about 2 minutes. Add the eggs one at a time, beating well after each. Alternately add the dry ingredients and the buttermilk mixture and beat until just combined. Add the apples and stir until evenly coated in batter. Pour into the prepared pan and smooth the top with a rubber spatula. Sprinkle evenly with the raspberries and bake until a toothpick inserted in the middle comes out clean, about 1 hour 20 minutes. Let cool completely, then cut into wedges to serve, either plain or dolloped with large mounds of whipped cream.

# Peanut Butter Cup Smith Island Cake

MAKES ONE 9-INCH LAYER CAKE

Smith Island cakes, traditional multilayered cakes from said island in Maryland, are beauties to behold: Eight pancake-thin layers of cake sandwich fudge frosting. Though you need to be careful when stacking the layers, it's okay if it looks lumpy; poured fudge frosting forgives all sins.

FOR THE CAKE:

3½ cups all-purpose flour

4 teaspoons baking powder

1½ teaspoons kosher salt

1½ cups (3 sticks) unsalted butter, melted

2¼ cups sugar

1½ cups milk

1 tablespoon vanilla extract

6 large eggs

½ cup peanut butter

FOR THE ICING:

8 ounces bittersweet chocolate, melted

4 cups sugar

2 cups evaporated milk

12 tablespoons (1½ sticks) unsalted butter, melted

1 tablespoon vanilla extract

1 teaspoon salt

½ cup finely chopped roasted and salted peanuts

MAKE THE CAKE: Heat the oven to 350°F. Spray four 9-inch round cake pans evenly with baking spray.

In a large bowl, whisk together the flour, baking powder, and salt. In another bowl, whisk together the butter, sugar, milk, vanilla, and eggs. Pour the wet ingredients over the dry ingredients and whisk until evenly combined. Let sit for 15 minutes, then stir again until smooth. Divide half of the batter among the four prepared pans, tilting the pans around so the batter covers the entire bottom. Bake, rotating the pans halfway through, until barely browned, about 15 minutes (they should look like pancakes from a skillet, slightly browned at the edges but still pale in the middle). Let cool in the pans for 20 minutes, then invert onto wire racks and let cool completely. Spray the pans again, divide the remaining batter among them, and repeat the baking and cooling process.

MAKE THE ICING: Once all of the layers have cooled completely, make the icing: Put half of each ingredient in a bowl and the other half in a medium-size saucepan. Bring the ingredients in the saucepan to a boil over medium-high heat and cook, stirring steadily, until the sugar is dissolved and the mixture is smooth and shiny, about 8 minutes. Remove from the heat and let sit until thick enough to spread, about 30 minutes. Place one cake on a cake stand or platter and, using an offset spatula or butter knife, spread with about a heaping ¼ cup icing to reach the edges; repeat with the remaining cakes and icing, leaving the top cake un-iced. Refrigerate the stacked cake to set the icing between the cakes, about 20 minutes. Pour the remaining ingredients in the bowl into a clean medium-size saucepan and repeat cooking as before. Let sit until thick enough to spread, about 30 minutes, then quickly spread over the top and sides of the cake (because the cake is chilled, the icing will set faster, so do this quickly and don't pause once you begin icing the cake).

Sprinkle the cake with the chopped peanuts, and let the icing on the outside cool and set before slicing and serving.

# "Red Velvet" Cake

MAKES ONE 8-INCH LAYER CAKE

When I was developing this cake for the book, I tried making a red velvet cake with no food coloring, since it's both a taboo ingredient for some and also causes allergic reactions in many of my friends. Beet juice is typically used, but I personally don't like its flavor in this cake. Instead I went for the next thing I could think of that might impart a blood-red hue to the cocoa-tinged cake: pomegranate juice. I reduced it by half to concentrate its flavor and color, and it was a success! It lends a pleasantly tart flavor that, along with the cocoa and tangy buttermilk, balances the sweetness of the cake, especially against the traditional whipped cream frosting (a slight misnomer since there's no cream in the actual recipe)—no cream cheese icing here, please. If you want it to be traditionally deep red, then simply add 2 tablespoons red food coloring, but if you prefer an all-natural, albeit slightly maroon-ish colored cake, then make this and surprise yourself with how good it is without the makeup.

---

FOR THE CAKE:

1 cup pomegranate juice

2½ cups cake flour, sifted

2 tablespoons natural cocoa powder, sifted

1 tablespoon baking powder

1 teaspoon kosher salt

½ cup buttermilk

1 tablespoon distilled white vinegar

1 teaspoon vanilla extract

1 cup (2 sticks) unsalted butter, softened

1½ cups sugar

2 large eggs

FOR THE FROSTING:

1½ cups sugar

⅓ cup all-purpose flour

1½ cups milk

1½ cups (3 sticks) unsalted butter, softened

2 teaspoons vanilla extract

MAKE THE CAKE: Heat the oven to 350°F. Spray three 8-inch round cake pans evenly with baking spray.

In a small saucepan, bring the pomegranate juice to a boil and cook until it is reduced by half; remove from the heat and let cool completely.

In a bowl, whisk together the flour, cocoa powder, baking powder, and salt. In another bowl, whisk together the buttermilk, reduced pomegranate juice, vinegar, and vanilla. In the bowl of a stand mixer fitted with the paddle attachment, beat the butter and sugar on medium-high speed until pale and fluffy, about 3 minutes. Add the eggs one at a time, beating well after each until smooth. Alternately add the dry ingredients and buttermilk mixture and beat until just combined. Divide the batter among the prepared pans and smooth the top with a rubber spatula. Drop the pans lightly on the counter to expel any large air bubbles. Bake until a toothpick inserted in the middle comes out clean, about 25 minutes. Let cool in the pans for 20 minutes, then invert the cakes onto wire racks to cool completely.

MAKE THE FROSTING: In a medium-size saucepan, whisk together the sugar and flour until evenly combined. Add the milk and whisk until smooth. Stirring often, bring to a boil over medium-high heat and cook, stirring constantly, until the mixture is the consistency of a smooth pudding, about 5 minutes (the paste is technically thick enough and ready as soon as it begins boiling, but you want to cook the raw flour taste out of the paste, so you must cook it for at least 5 minutes). Remove the pudding from the heat and let cool to room temperature.

In the bowl of a stand mixer fitted with the paddle attachment, beat the butter and one fourth of the pudding on medium-high speed until fluffy and smooth, about 1 minute. Add half of the remaining pudding, beat until smooth, then add the remaining pudding and the vanilla. Increase the speed to high and beat the frosting until white and fluffy, about 5 minutes. Place one cake on a cake stand and spread with 1 cup of the frosting. Place a second cake over the frosting and spread with another cup of frosting. Top with the third cake, then cover the top and sides with the remaining frosting. Refrigerate the cake to firm the frosting, about 1 hour. Let come to room temperature again before serving.

# Sour Cream Cheesecake

MAKES ONE 9-INCH CAKE

When I was growing up, this was always my birthday cake. I never liked traditional yellow cake with vanilla frosting, much preferring this deep, dense, rich cheesecake (the one time of the year I ever ate it). My mom would make it for me, and I would have it every day for the rest of the week as a cooling snack after being out in the blistering August heat; it seemed to get better and better each day. It's intensely, unapologetically rich, and tinged with sour cream, which adds extra tang to the sweet filling.

---

1⅓ cups vanilla wafer crumbs (about 40 cookies)

½ cup (1 stick) unsalted butter, melted and cooled

½ cup chopped pecans

⅓ cup confectioners' sugar

5 (8-ounce) packages cream cheese, softened

1¾ cups granulated sugar

3 tablespoons all-purpose flour

1 teaspoon kosher salt

1 teaspoon vanilla extract

5 large eggs, at room temperature

2 large egg yolks, at room temperature

1 cup sour cream

Heat the oven to 450°F.

In a food processor, combine the vanilla wafer crumbs, butter, pecans, and confectioners' sugar and process until very finely ground. Transfer to a 9-inch springform pan and press evenly into the bottom. Wrap the outside of the pan with aluminum foil.

Put the cream cheese in the bowl of a stand mixer fitted with the paddle attachment and beat on medium-high speed until fluffy, about 2 minutes. Add the granulated sugar, flour, salt, and vanilla and beat until smooth. Add the eggs and yolks one at a time, beating well after each, then stir in the sour cream. Pour the batter over the crust and bake for 10 minutes. Lower the oven temperature to 250°F and continue to bake until the filling is almost set and slightly loose in the center when tapped on the side, about 1 hour more. Turn the oven off and leave the cake in the oven until completely cool, 2 to 3 hours. Transfer the cheesecake in the pan to the refrigerator and chill for at least 8 hours or overnight to set.

Remove foil and sides of springform pan before serving. Wrap leftover cake tightly and keep in the refrigerator for up to 1 week.

# Southern Cassata

MAKES ONE 12-INCH CAKE

Cassata is a traditional Sicilian Easter dessert of sponge cake filled with sweet ricotta, the whole thing cloaked in marzipan and decorated with candied fruits. It's a beauty to behold and benefits from being made a couple of days ahead to give it plenty of time to set up. In my version, I use cream cheese in place of ricotta and cover the cake in toasted pecan marzipan instead of the traditional almond or pistachio. A decoration of bananas, coconut, and pecans makes this Bourbon-soaked cake a celebration of the South's greatest dessert ingredients.

---

FOR THE CAKE:

¾ cup sugar

Grated zest of ½ lemon

6 large eggs

1¼ cups all-purpose flour

½ teaspoon kosher salt

FOR THE PECAN MARZIPAN:

1 cup roughly chopped pecans

1 cup confectioners' sugar, plus more for the work surface

1 large egg white, lightly beaten

FOR THE FILLING AND SYRUP:

12 ounces cream cheese

½ cup sugar

1 teaspoon vanilla extract

½ teaspoon ground cinnamon

½ teaspoon kosher salt

2 tablespoons Bourbon

FOR THE GLAZE AND GARNISH:

2 cups confectioners' sugar

2 tablespoons plus 2 teaspoons fresh lemon juice

Whole pecan halves, toasted and cooled

Banana slices

Toasted shaved coconut

MAKE THE CAKE: Heat the oven to 350°F. Spray a 9-inch round cake pan evenly with baking spray.

In a bowl, combine the sugar, lemon zest, and eggs and beat with a handheld mixer on high speed until pale and light, about 5 minutes. Sprinkle the flour and salt over the egg mixture and carefully fold until just combined. Pour into the prepared pan and smooth the top with a rubber spatula. Bake until a toothpick inserted in the middle comes out clean and the top is light golden brown, about 30 minutes. Let cool in the pan for 20 minutes, then invert onto a wire rack and let cool completely. Using a serrated knife, cut the cake into wide strips. The cake can be prepared to this point up to 2 days in advance; place the strips on a parchment paper–lined baking sheet and wrap in plastic wrap.

MAKE THE MARZIPAN: Line the bottom and side of a 12-inch pie plate or other shallow round dish with plastic wrap, letting plenty of excess hang over the side. Put the pecans in a food processor and process until finely ground. Add

the confectioners' sugar and continue processing until very finely ground. Add about half of the egg white and process until the mixture forms a ball of dough; you will not need all of the egg white. You want the marzipan dough to be smooth and moist enough to work with but not sticky. If it's still too dry, add another teaspoon of the egg white until it reaches the perfect consistency, like that of barely moist Play-Doh. When the marzipan is just right, transfer it to a work surface dusted with confectioners' sugar and knead it a couple more times until it stays in a smooth ball. Using a rolling pin dusted with more confectioners' sugar, roll the marzipan into a 6-by-12-inch rectangle about ¼ inch thick. Cut the marzipan lengthwise into strips 2 inches wide and line the side of the pie plate with the strips, flattening where they overlap to form one continuous ring (if the side of your dish is deeper than 2 inches, cut the strips as wide as needed to fit the side snugly).

MAKE THE FILLING AND SYRUP: In a bowl, combine the cream cheese, ¼ cup of the sugar, the vanilla, cinnamon, and salt and beat with a handheld mixer on medium-high speed until smooth and fluffy, about 3 minutes.

In a saucepan, bring the remaining ¼ cup sugar and ¼ cup water to a boil, stirring until the sugar dissolves, then remove from the heat and stir in the Bourbon. Let the syrup cool completely.

ASSEMBLE THE CASSATA: Line the bottom of the marzipan-lined pie plate with the smaller cake strips, cutting them to fit while letting their edges rest over the marzipan so there are no gaps between the marzipan and cake. Drizzle the cake

with about ¼ cup of the Bourbon syrup, then spoon the filling on top, spreading it evenly to cover the cake, then smooth the top with a rubber spatula. Cover the filling with the remaining cake strips, cutting them to fit evenly. (You will have a couple scraps of cake left over: Snack on them!) Drizzle the cake with the remaining Bourbon syrup. If any part of the marzipan sticks above the level of the cake strips, fold it over onto the cake, then fold the plastic overhang over the whole cake and cover with more plastic wrap. Refrigerate the cassata to set the ingredients together into a snug whole, at least 4 hours, but ideally overnight.

About 1 hour before you're ready to serve the cassata, make a glaze by stirring together the confectioners' sugar and 2 tablespoons of the lemon juice in a small bowl. This glaze will be pretty thick, but you want it to be just spreadable, not runny at all. If it's too thick to stir, add another 1 teaspoon of juice. Unwrap the cassata and place a serving platter upside down over the pie plate, then flip them together, letting the cassata fall onto the platter. Carefully remove the pie plate and plastic wrap, then pour the glaze onto the middle of the cake. Using an offset spatula or butter knife, carefully spread the glaze until it covers the cake strips on the top of the cake; you don't want it to run over the sides onto the marzipan. It will seem impossible at first, but work patiently and slowly, and the glaze will just touch the marzipan perfectly and stay put. Refrigerate the cake again to set the glaze, at least another 30 minutes.

When ready to serve, decorate the top with pecans, banana slices, and a pile of toasted coconut.

# Sweet Potato Cake

MAKES ONE 8-INCH LAYER CAKE

My favorite Thanksgiving side dish is sweet potato casserole the way my aunt Barbara Jane makes it. I can never get enough of the rich, smooth sweet potatoes, topped with a crunchy cashew crust. But it always seems more like dessert than a side dish. Here, I transform it fully into a dessert, and what a showstopper: three thick layers of sweet potato cake, stacked very high with a homemade marshmallow meringue filling with toasted pecans and drizzled with a praline-like caramel sauce. It's as decadent and over-the-top as the side dish, but no longer in the turkey's shadow.

---

FOR THE CAKE:

1 cup (2 sticks) unsalted butter

3 cups all-purpose flour

1 tablespoon baking powder

½ teaspoon baking soda

1 teaspoon kosher salt

1½ teaspoons ground cinnamon

1½ teaspoons ground ginger

¾ teaspoon ground cardamom

¼ teaspoon ground allspice

2 cups packed light brown sugar

4 large eggs

2 cups mashed roasted sweet potatoes

¾ cup sour cream

1½ teaspoons vanilla extract

MAKE THE CAKE: In a small saucepan, melt the butter over medium-high heat and cook, stirring, until it begins to smell nutty and the solids brown lightly. Pour into a small heatproof bowl and refrigerate until solid, about 1 hour.

Heat the oven to 350°F. Spray three 8-inch round cake pans evenly with baking spray.

In a bowl, whisk together the flour, baking powder, baking soda, salt, cinnamon, ginger, cardamom, and allspice. Put the browned butter and brown sugar in the bowl of a stand mixer fitted with the paddle attachment and beat on medium-high speed until smooth and fluffy, about 4 minutes. Add the eggs one at a time, beating until smooth after each. Add the sweet potatoes, sour cream, and vanilla and beat until smooth. Add the dry ingredients and beat until just combined and smooth. Divide the batter among the prepared pans and smooth the tops with a rubber spatula. Bake until a toothpick inserted in the middle of each comes out clean, 35 to 40 minutes. Let cool for 20 minutes, then invert onto wire racks and let cool completely. (The cakes can be made up to 1 day in advance; wrap in plastic wrap and keep at room temperature.)

**FOR THE MARSHMALLOW MERINGUE:**

2 large egg whites

1 cup sugar

¼ teaspoon kosher salt

½ teaspoon vanilla extract

**FOR THE CANDIED PECANS:**

4 tablespoons (½ stick) unsalted butter

¼ cup sugar

¼ cup dark rum

2¼ cups whole pecan halves, toasted and cooled

**FOR THE PRALINE SAUCE:**

1 cup confectioners' sugar

¾ cup packed light brown sugar

6 tablespoons (¾ stick) unsalted butter, melted

¼ cup milk

½ teaspoon kosher salt

½ teaspoon vanilla extract

MAKE THE MARSHMALLOW MERINGUE: Put the egg whites in a large, heavy bowl and beat with a handheld mixer on high speed until frothy, about 1 minute. In a small saucepan, bring the sugar, salt, and ½ cup water to a boil over high heat, stirring to dissolve the sugar. When the mixture comes to a boil, quit stirring and attach a candy thermometer to the side of the pan; continue cooking until the syrup reaches 250°F. Remove the pan from the heat, remove the thermometer, then begin beating the egg whites again on high speed. With the handheld mixer in one hand, hold the saucepan of syrup with the other (or have someone help you if you're not ambidextrous) and slowly pour the hot syrup in a steady stream into the whites while beating them. Once the syrup is all added, add the vanilla and continue beating until the mixture triples in volume and is barely warm to the touch; it will form stiff peaks as well. Divide the meringue evenly among the three cooled cakes and use an offset spatula or butter knife to spread the meringue over each cake evenly, leaving a 1-inch border at the edges of two of the cakes and taking the meringue just to the edge of the third cake (the first two cakes will be the bottom and middle layers of the cake and you want to leave room for the meringue to spread under the pressure of the other cakes without gushing out the sides). Let cool while you make the candied pecans.

MAKE THE CANDIED PECANS: Heat the butter in a 12-inch skillet over medium-high heat until melted. Add the sugar, rum, and pecans and cook, stirring often, until the pecans are thickly glazed, about 4 minutes. Transfer to a sheet of aluminum foil and spread into an even layer. Let cool completely, then break the pecans apart and sprinkle them evenly among the meringue-frosted cakes. Place one of the first two cakes on a cake stand or serving platter and top with the second cake. Place the third cake on top and then refrigerate the whole cake to help it set, at least 1 hour.

MAKE THE PRALINE SAUCE: Bring the confectioners' sugar, brown sugar, butter, milk, salt, and vanilla to a boil in a small saucepan, stirring often, over high heat and cook until smooth, 4 to 5 minutes. Remove from the heat and let cool, without stirring, until thickened, about 15 minutes. Stir the sauce until smooth, then drizzle over the cake; refrigerate until ready to serve. Serve the cake at room temperature with more sauce.

# Sweet & Smoky Snack Cake

I entered this strange-sounding little number in a bacon-cooking contest one summer in New York City. Its inspiration was Devils on Horseback, those retro appetizers of chutney-stuffed prunes wrapped in bacon. I steeped some prunes in black tea and citrus zest, pureed them into a cake made with bacon fat instead of butter, and topped it off with a quince chutney. To my chagrin, no one knew what devils on horseback were, so no one got the reference or wondered why I was serving them a bacon-flavored cake. Fortunately, no one needs a reason to enjoy a cake made with bacon; it sells itself. This cake has the texture of a fresh gingerbread or honey cake and a pleasant smokiness from the bacon fat—neither too overwhelming nor too subtle.

---

1 pound pitted prunes

1½ cups brewed strong black tea, such as English Breakfast or Earl Grey (I used 3 tea bags)

¼ cup Cognac or brandy

Grated zest of 1 orange

Grated zest of 1 lemon

Grated zest of 1 lime

1 cup rendered bacon fat, chilled solid

1½ cups packed dark brown sugar

4 large eggs

1 teaspoon vanilla extract

2½ cups all-purpose flour

1 tablespoon baking powder

1 teaspoon kosher salt

¼ teaspoon ground cinnamon

¼ teaspoon ground mace

In a medium-size saucepan, combine the prunes, tea, Cognac, and citrus zests. Bring to a boil, then simmer, covered, for 10 minutes. Remove from the heat and let sit until cooled to room temperature and the prunes have soaked up all the liquid. Puree in a food processor until smooth.

Heat the oven to 350°F. Spray a 9-by-13-inch baking dish evenly with baking spray.

In a bowl, combine the bacon fat and brown sugar and beat with a handheld mixer on medium-high speed until fluffy and smooth, about 4 minutes. Add the eggs one at a time, beating well after each until smooth. Add the pureed prunes and the vanilla and beat until smooth. In a separate bowl, whisk together the flour, baking powder, salt, cinnamon, and mace until evenly combined, then add to the prune mixture and beat on low speed until just combined.

Pour the batter into the prepared baking dish and smooth the top with a rubber spatula. Bake until a toothpick inserted in the middle comes out clean, 40 to 45 minutes. Let cool completely, then cut into squares to serve.

# Walnut Spice Cake

MAKES ONE 9-INCH LAYER CAKE

This cake is a stunner. Alternating layers of spiced cake and stark white cake sandwiched and enveloped in a dark fudge icing and sprinkled with walnuts. It's an old-fashioned beauty, originally included in a story about southern layer cakes I wrote for *Saveur*.

FOR THE CAKE:

3 cups cake flour

2½ teaspoons baking powder

1 teaspoon kosher salt

1 cup milk

1 teaspoon vanilla extract

1½ teaspoons ground cinnamon

1 teaspoon ground allspice

½ teaspoon ground cloves

1 cup vegetable shortening (see Note)

2 cups sugar

6 large egg whites, at room temperature

FOR THE ICING:

4 cups sugar

3 cups milk

¾ cup (1½ sticks) unsalted butter, melted

⅓ cup Dutch-process cocoa powder, sifted

2 teaspoons vanilla extract

1 teaspoon baking soda

2 cups whole walnut halves

MAKE THE CAKE: Heat the oven to 350°F. Spray two 9-inch round cake pans evenly with baking spray.

In a bowl, combine the flour, baking powder, and salt. In a glass measuring cup, combine the milk and vanilla. In a small bowl, combine the cinnamon, allspice, and cloves. In the bowl of a stand mixer fitted with the paddle attachment, combine the shortening and sugar and beat until light and fluffy, about 3 minutes. Add the egg whites one at a time, beating well after each until the batter is smooth. Turn the mixer speed to low and alternately add the dry ingredients and milk mixture, beginning and ending with the dry ingredients, and beat until just combined and smooth. Pour half of the batter into one of the prepared cake pans, then stir the spice mixture into the other half; pour the spiced cake batter into the other cake pan. Smooth the tops of the cakes and give the pans a good bang on the counter to settle the batter evenly into the pans.

Bake, rotating the cake pans halfway through baking, until lightly browned at the edges and a toothpick inserted in the middle comes out clean, about 30 minutes. Let cool in the pans for 25 minutes, then invert onto wire racks and let cool completely. Split each cake horizontally in half with a serrated knife. (The cakes can be made to this point up to 1 day in advance; wrap in plastic wrap and keep at room temperature.)

MAKE THE ICING: In a 6-quart copper saucepan or Dutch oven (see Tip, page 20), combine the sugar, milk, butter, and cocoa powder and attach a candy thermometer to the side of the pan. Cook over medium heat, stirring constantly from the bottom with a wooden spoon to prevent scorching, until the mixture reaches 234°F, about 30 minutes. Remove from the heat and immediately add the vanilla and baking soda; stir until smooth, then let sit for 1 minute. Using a handheld mixer, beat the icing on medium speed until it reaches the consistency of loose pudding, 1 to 2 minutes. Working quickly, place one spiced cake on a cake stand and evenly pour about ½ cup of the icing over the surface of the cake (eyeball this amount; it doesn't need to be exact and pouring the icing into a measuring cup and then back out will only slow you down). Place a plain cake on top and evenly pour about another ½ cup of the icing over the surface of the cake. Place the second spiced cake on top and cover with another ½ cup icing. Top with the second plain cake, then steadily and evenly pour the remaining icing over the cake, trying to disperse it evenly while pouring. Quickly spread the icing falling over the sides of the cake over the other layers until it covers the sides completely. Sprinkle the top with the walnuts, pressing them lightly into the icing to stick, then let the icing cool completely to set before serving. Store any remaining cake at room temperature, covered in a cake dome or loosely wrapped in plastic wrap, for up to 5 days.

## Good to Know: VEGETABLE SHORTENING

Don't be put off by the vegetable shortening here; it maintains the pure white color of the cake. Good-quality, all-natural organic shortenings are widely available (I like Spectrum Naturals), but if you prefer to use butter, simply substitute an equal amount of room-temperature unsalted butter.

# Pies & Tarts

BANANA PUDDING PIE

BLUEBERRY-RASPBERRY JAM PIE

CHOCOLATE-RASPBERRY GANACHE TART

*CAMOTES* PIE

CHOCOLATE CHESS PIE

CHOCOLATE CREAM PIE

FIG TART

FRIED HAND PIES

LEMON ICEBOX TART

PEANUT BUTTER–APPLE TART

LEMON MERINGUE PIE

PEACH COBBLER

PEANUT BUTTER PIE

PECAN PIE

PECAN-CRANBERRY LINZER TORTE

PERSIMMON PIE

PINEAPPLE TARTE TATIN

PUMPKIN *KANAFE*

SHAKER KEY LIME PIE

TREACLE CASHEW TART

TRIPLE CHERRY PIE

# Banana Pudding Pie

MAKES ONE 9-INCH DEEP-DISH PIE

Banana pudding—a southern classic—was one of the first recipes I took a stab at modernizing. My favorite version used pecan shortbread cookies instead of the iconic Nilla wafers, so when I decided to make banana pudding as a pie I made it with a pecan shortbread crust. At the time, I had been obsessively making a banana caramel sauce from Sherry Yard's *The Secrets of Baking* and thought it'd be a great complement to the traditional vanilla pudding and whipped cream in this update. Together with the fresh bananas, this recipe became a southern-accented hybrid of banana pudding and British banoffee pie, a layered treat of caramel, bananas, and whipped cream in a pastry crust. It just goes to show that no matter what great idea you come up with, it's likely someone has already done it.

FOR THE VANILLA PUDDING:

¼ cup sugar

2 tablespoons cornstarch

½ teaspoon kosher salt

½ vanilla bean, seeds scraped and reserved

4 large egg yolks

1 cup milk

FOR THE PECAN SHORTBREAD CRUST:

¾ cup whole pecan halves

¼ cup sugar

1½ cups all-purpose flour, plus more for the work surface

½ teaspoon kosher salt

½ cup (1 stick) cold unsalted butter, cut into cubes

⅓ cup ice-cold water

MAKE THE VANILLA PUDDING: In a small saucepan, whisk the sugar, cornstarch, and salt together until evenly combined. Add the vanilla bean and seeds and the egg yolks and whisk until well combined. Add the milk, whisk well, then place over medium heat and bring to a simmer, stirring often. Simmer, stirring constantly, until the mixture has thickened to the consistency of loose pudding, about 2 minutes. Pour into a bowl and press a piece of plastic wrap directly onto the surface of the pudding. Let cool to room temperature, then refrigerate until chilled and set, at least 4 hours or up to 1 day.

MAKE THE PECAN SHORTBREAD CRUST: In a food processor, combine the pecans and sugar and process until very finely ground. Add the flour and salt and process until evenly combined. Add the butter and pulse until pea-size crumbles form and it's evenly incorporated, about 10 pulses. Add the water and pulse until the dough begins to form and stick together. Transfer to a work surface and form into a ball; flatten into a disk and wrap with plastic wrap. Refrigerate the dough for 1 hour.

Heat the oven to 375°F. Unwrap the dough disk and transfer it to a floured work surface. Using a floured rolling pin, roll the dough into a ¼-inch-thick round at least 13 inches in diameter. Transfer to a 9-inch deep-dish pie pan and press lightly into the bottom

2 tablespoons unsalted butter

¼ cup granulated sugar

¼ cup packed light brown sugar

½ teaspoon kosher salt

2 very ripe bananas, peeled
and mashed

2 tablespoons dark rum

1 tablespoon fresh lemon juice

TO ASSEMBLE:

2 ripe bananas, peeled and cut
crosswise into ¼-inch-thick coins

1 cup heavy cream

½ cup confectioners' sugar

½ teaspoon vanilla extract

Cocoa powder (optional)

and side. Trim the excess from the edge, then poke the bottom of the pastry with the tines of a fork. Place a sheet of aluminum foil or parchment paper over the pastry and fill with pie weights. Bake until the crust is beginning to set and the edge begins to brown, about 15 minutes. Remove the foil and weights and continue to bake until golden brown and the crust is cooked through, about 10 minutes more. Let cool completely. (The crust can be made to this point up to 1 day in advance; wrap in plastic wrap and keep at room temperature.)

MAKE THE BANANA CARAMEL SAUCE: Melt the butter in a small skillet over medium-high heat. Add both sugars and the salt and stir constantly with a wooden spoon until the sugar is evenly moistened in the butter and the mixture is melted and molten (the sugar will not dissolve fully). Add the bananas, rum, and lemon juice and cook, stirring, until the mixture is bubbly and evenly combined, at least 2 minutes. Remove from the heat and transfer to a bowl. Let cool completely to room temperature, stirring every few minutes. (If making in advance, cover with plastic wrap and store in the refrigerator; let the sauce come to room temperature before proceeding with the recipe.)

When the caramel has cooled, remove the pudding from the refrigerator and whisk until smooth again. Add to the caramel sauce and use a rubber spatula to fold the pudding and sauce together until almost combined (you still want to have some streaks of sauce in the pudding). Pour into the shortbread crust and smooth the top with a rubber spatula. Cover the pudding with the fresh banana coins.

In a bowl, combine the cream, confectioners' sugar, and vanilla and whisk until stiff peaks form. Pour the cream over the bananas and pudding and spread to the edge of the pie, smoothing the top and creating peaks and valleys in the whipped cream. Refrigerate the pie until set, at least 2 hours. Before serving, dust the top of the pie lightly with cocoa powder, if you like.

# Blueberry-Raspberry Jam Pie

MAKES ONE 9-INCH DEEP-DISH PIE

I love blueberries most when their natural sweetness is tamed by something tart, such as lemon or, as in this recipe, raspberries. Between the berries themselves and the preserves, there's no need for much more sugar. With just a little orange juice and zest to brighten things up, and a beautiful lattice top, this humble pie becomes a showstopper.

---

Double batch (2 disks) Pastry Dough (page 81)

¼ cup cornstarch

2 tablespoons sugar

½ teaspoon kosher salt

Grated zest of ½ orange

1 tablespoon fresh orange juice

1 teaspoon vanilla extract

1 cup raspberry preserves, store-bought or homemade (see page 68)

3 pounds blueberries

Egg wash (see page 80)

Coarse sanding sugar (optional)

Heat the oven to 375°F. Line a baking sheet with parchment paper.

Roll one dough disk out into a round ¼ inch thick and line a 9-inch deep-dish pie pan with it. Roll the other disk out into a round ¼-inch thick and place it on the prepared baking sheet. Using a pizza cutter or paring knife, cut the dough into ¾-inch-thick strips; refrigerate the strips and the dough-lined pie pan while you make the filling.

In a bowl, whisk together the cornstarch, sugar, and salt. Add the orange zest, juice, and vanilla, then add the preserves. Stir in the blueberries until they're evenly coated with the preserves. Pour the berries into the lined pie pan, mounding them to fit. Using the strips of dough, form a lattice top over the berries, either by weaving the strips or arranging them on top of each other in a crisscross pattern. Press the strips into the dough at the edge of the pan and trim the edges. Fold the edges underneath themselves and press them lightly back onto the pie pan. Brush all the exposed dough with some egg wash and sprinkle with some coarse sanding sugar, if you want.

Place the pie pan on the baking sheet and bake until the juices are bubbling in the center and the dough is golden brown and cooked through, about 1 hour. If the pastry is done, but the filling has yet to bubble, lay a piece of aluminum foil over the pie until the filling is ready. Let the pie cool completely to set before slicing and serving.

# FRUIT PRESERVES

I love fruit jams and preserves just as much as the next person, and I especially love making them for myself so I know exactly what goes into them. But when I first started making my own, I got intimidated by all the rigorous formulas involving pectin and other gelling ingredients. While using pectin, a chemical in certain fruits that acts like a starch to set liquids, is necessary when making clear jellies, I knew that I could achieve the ideal setting texture by playing with the proportions of liquid and sugar in the jam, cooking it to a point where, when cooled, it would set to the consistency I wanted. My formula is this: Weigh your fruit, be it berries, chopped apples, or figs, then divide that weight by three. The resulting number is the weight of sugar you should use. Further, divide this number by three, and this will give you the weight of lemon juice, which will cut through the necessary amount of sugar, balancing the jam with acidity. Depending on the fruit, I'll also add half a spent vanilla bean or a cinnamon stick to impart a fragrant spice note. I also add a hefty pinch of salt, proportional to the amount of fruit and sugar I'm using. You can also use different sweeteners with this formula (I love to use half honey and sugar when making fig jam, for example) to further enhance the flavors of your fruit. Here's the basic recipe for the raspberry preserves I use in my Blueberry-Raspberry Jam Tart (page 67) and Chocolate-Raspberry Ganache Tart (page 69). I substitute cherries for my Triple Cherry Pie (page 107) and cranberries in my Pecan-Cranberry Linzer Torte (page 93).

---

1 pound fresh or thawed raspberries

10 tablespoons sugar

2½ tablespoons fresh lemon juice

¼ spent vanilla bean

½ teaspoon kosher salt

In a medium saucepan, combine the raspberries, sugar, lemon juice, vanilla bean, and salt and stir until evenly combined. Let sit for about 10 minutes to allow the sugar to pull some juices from the raspberries. Place the pan over medium-low heat and cover the pan. Cook, stirring occasionally, until the raspberries are very soft, about 20 minutes. Uncover, increase the heat to medium-high, and cook, stirring often, until the raspberries are broken down and beginning to stick to the bottom of the pan (this is your indication that the jam will set at the right consistency; cook it further if you want a thicker jam, but stir constantly, as the jam will stick and burn immediately if left unattended). Remove from the heat and let cool; if you want a smooth jam, puree the cooled jam in a food processor. Transfer to a glass jar and put the lid on. Store in the refrigerator for up to 2 weeks.

# Chocolate-Raspberry Ganache Tart

MAKES ONE 4-BY-14-INCH RECTANGULAR TART

In desserts as simple as this, the quality of ingredients really makes the difference in the final product. I prefer Valrhona chocolate for all my baking, but any good-quality, preferably fair-trade, brand will do. Same with the raspberry preserves: The better the quality, the more outstanding your tart will taste. Desserts like this lend themselves to elaborate presentations, so be emboldened to use over-the-top decorative tart molds, or fancy piping tips for the whipped cream.

---

FOR THE CRUST:

½ cup (1 stick) unsalted butter, softened

¼ cup sugar

¾ teaspoon vanilla extract

¼ teaspoon kosher salt

1 cup all-purpose flour

FOR THE GANACHE:

8 ounces bittersweet chocolate, finely chopped

½ cup heavy cream

½ cup raspberry preserves, store-bought or homemade (page 68)

TO ASSEMBLE:

1 cup heavy cream

¼ cup confectioners' sugar, sifted

2 tablespoons Chambord (black raspberry liqueur)

MAKE THE CRUST: In a bowl, combine the butter, sugar, vanilla, and salt and beat with a handheld mixer on medium-high speed until pale and fluffy, 2 to 3 minutes. Add the flour and beat until just combined. Transfer the dough to a 4-by-14-inch rectangular tart pan with a removable bottom and press it evenly into the bottom and up the sides; refrigerate for at least 30 minutes.

Heat the oven to 350°F.

Prick the dough all over with the tines of a fork and bake until set and golden brown, about 25 minutes. Let cool completely.

MAKE THE GANACHE: Put the chocolate in a heatproof bowl and set a fine-mesh sieve over the bowl. In a small saucepan, heat the cream and preserves over medium-high heat, stirring to dissolve the preserves, until they begin to simmer. Remove from the heat and pour through the sieve into the bowl with the chocolate, pressing any solid pieces of preserves through the strainer; let the chocolate and cream sit for 1 minute. Using a rubber spatula, slowly stir until smooth and shiny. Pour into the cooled crust and refrigerate until set.

Whisk together the cream, confectioners' sugar, and Chambord in a bowl until stiff peaks form. Transfer to a piping bag fitted with a medium star tip and pipe it decoratively over the filling, if you like, or simply spread the whipped cream over the top of the tart. Cut into wedges or bars to serve.

# Camotes Pie

This pie came about from one of those "duh!" moments. I was in Morelia, Mexico, years ago, eating *camotes*, a candied dessert of sweet potatoes or pumpkin stewed in a fragrant syrup of *piloncillo* (Mexican raw brown sugar), orange juice, and cinnamon. I was eating and thinking the whole time that it tasted of the sweet potato pies from back home. The *piloncillo* lends a musky depth lacking from granulated sugar or even American brown sugar, and the orange juice and cinnamon lighten and spice up the sweet potatoes. When pureed into a smooth filling, or even left somewhat chunky for a more rustic texture, it's an ideal filling for pumpkin or sweet potato pie, with just a slight nod to our neighbors across the Gulf.

---

Single batch (1 disk) Pastry Dough (page 81)

8 ounces *piloncillo* sugar, roughly chopped, or 1 cup packed dark brown or muscovado sugar

½ cup fresh orange juice

1 pound sweet potatoes, peeled and cut into 1-inch chunks

1 stick cinnamon, preferably Mexican canela

1 (1-inch) piece fresh ginger, peeled and finely grated

Grated zest of 1 orange

2 large eggs

1 tablespoon cornstarch

1 teaspoon kosher salt

3 tablespoons granulated sugar (optional)

¼ teaspoon ground cinnamon (optional)

Roll the dough out into a round ¼ inch thick and line a 9-inch deep-dish pie pan with it, trimming the edges. Place on a parchment paper–lined baking sheet and refrigerate until ready to use.

In a large saucepan, heat the *piloncillo*, orange juice, and ½ cup water over medium-high heat, stirring often, until dissolved, 10 minutes. Add the sweet potatoes, cinnamon stick, ginger, and orange zest. Lower the heat to medium-low, cover, and cook, stirring occasionally, until the sweet potatoes are very tender, about 30 minutes. Remove from the heat and let cool.

Heat the oven to 325°F.

Using a slotted spoon, transfer all the sweet potatoes to a food processor, then pour in 2 cups of the cooking syrup and puree until smooth. (Discard any remaining cooking liquid.) Add the eggs, cornstarch, and salt and puree until smooth. Pour into the pie shell and bake until the filling is set but still slightly wobbly in the center and the crust is lightly browned, about 45 minutes. Let cool completely to set the filling. You can serve this pie as is, or combine the granulated sugar and ground cinnamon, sprinkle it over the top of the pie, and brown it with a handheld torch to create a crisp, crème brûlée–like crust (see page 44) before slicing and serving.

# Chocolate Chess Pie

MAKES ONE 9-INCH PIE

Chess pie is a ubiquitous southern pie, seen at every church social, lunch counter, and buffet. My favorite is a chocolate version that a church lady would bring to country club luncheons in my town. Intensely chocolaty and eggy from the custard, it was a gleaming beauty, offset simply by a crisp, cracker-like piecrust and plain whipped cream. It's the stuff of a chocolate purist's dreams.

Single batch (1 disk) Pastry Dough (page 81)

1 cup packed light brown sugar

½ cup granulated sugar

½ cup Dutch-process cocoa powder

4 large egg yolks

2 large whole eggs

1 teaspoon kosher salt

½ teaspoon freshly grated nutmeg

¾ cup buttermilk

6 tablespoons (¾ stick) unsalted butter, melted and cooled

Heat the oven to 325°F.

Roll the dough out into a round ¼ inch thick and line a 9-inch pie pan with it, trimming the edges; refrigerate until ready to use.

In a bowl, whisk together the brown sugar, granulated sugar, and cocoa powder, then add the whole eggs and egg yolks, salt, and nutmeg and stir until smooth. Add the buttermilk and butter and stir until evenly combined. Pour into the pie shell, place on a baking sheet, and bake until the crust is golden brown and the filling is set but still jiggles slightly when shaken, about 45 minutes. Let cool completely before slicing.

# Chocolate Cream Pie

MAKES ONE 9-INCH DEEP-DISH PIE

I'll admit I'm not a frequent chocolate eater. However, when I do need a chocolate fix, it has to be a big one. This pie—super thick from rich chocolate pudding domed high above a crunchy chocolate wafer crust with just enough whipped cream on top—does the trick every time. Do note that in order for the pie to set firmly and cut cleanly, it should chill several hours in the fridge. No rushing: It's all about delayed gratification.

---

¾ cup granulated sugar

¼ cup cornstarch

1 teaspoon kosher salt

6 large egg yolks

2 cups half-and-half

1 cup (2 sticks) unsalted butter

8 ounces bittersweet chocolate, finely chopped, plus more for shaving

1½ teaspoons vanilla extract

2 tablespoons packed light brown sugar

1 (9-ounce) package chocolate wafer cookies, finely ground (about 2¼ cups)

2 cups heavy cream

In a medium-size saucepan, whisk together the granulated sugar, cornstarch, and salt, then add the egg yolks and whisk until smooth. Stir in the half-and-half and heat over medium heat, stirring often, until thickened to the consistency of loose pudding. Remove from the heat, add one third of ½ cup (1 stick) of the butter and one third of the chocolate, and whisk until smooth; repeat until the whole stick of butter and all of the chocolate are added. Stir in 1 teaspoon of the vanilla, then pour the pudding through a fine-mesh sieve into a bowl. Press a piece of plastic wrap onto the surface to prevent a skin from forming and let cool completely. Refrigerate until set, at least 4 hours.

Heat the oven to 375°F.

Heat the remaining ½ cup (1 stick) butter and the brown sugar in a small saucepan until the sugar is dissolved, add the ground wafers, and stir until the crumbs are evenly coated in butter. Transfer to a 9-inch deep-dish pie pan and press the crumbs into the bottom and up the sides, using the bottom of a measuring cup to compress the crust. Bake until the crumbs are set, about 15 minutes. Let cool completely.

Uncover the pudding and stir until smooth again. Pour into the crust, forming a dome, and smooth the top with a rubber spatula. In a large bowl, whisk the remaining ½ teaspoon vanilla and the cream until stiff peaks form, then spread the whipped cream on top of the pudding. Using a vegetable peeler, shave some chocolate over the pie. Refrigerate for at least 4 hours or up to overnight to set before serving.

# Fig Tart

MAKES ONE 4-BY-14-INCH RECTANGULAR TART

There's a special place in my heart reserved just for Fig Newtons. Despite being a pastry chef with a sweet tooth the size of a sugar mill, I've often limited my own intake of sweets, and during these periods of self-imposed exile Fig Newtons were the only treat I allowed myself. This homemade version tastes even better than my childhood favorite, without the artificial ingredients and preservatives found in processed foods.

---

8 ounces dried Mission figs, stemmed and quartered

2 cups brewed black tea

2 tablespoons Lyle's golden syrup (see page 113)

2 teaspoons fresh lemon juice

1 cup (2 sticks) unsalted butter, softened

½ cup sugar

1 tablespoon vanilla extract

1 teaspoon ground cinnamon

¼ teaspoon kosher salt

1¼ cups all-purpose flour

1 cup whole-wheat flour

In a medium-size saucepan, combine the figs, tea, syrup, and lemon juice and bring to a boil. Lower the heat to a simmer and cook, stirring, until the figs are very soft and barely any liquid remains, about 10 minutes. Transfer to a food processor and puree until smooth. Let cool completely while you make the dough.

Heat the oven to 350°F.

In the bowl of a stand mixer fitted with the paddle attachment, beat the butter, sugar, vanilla, cinnamon, and salt until fluffy. Add both flours and mix until just combined. Transfer three quarters of the dough to a 4-by-14-inch rectangular tart pan with a removable bottom and press it evenly into the bottom and up the sides to form thick sidewalls. Pour the fig filling over the dough, then break the remaining dough into large crumbles and sprinkle them over the filling until almost completely covered. Bake until golden brown and set, about 45 minutes. Let cool completely before cutting into bars.

# Fried Hand Pies

(CHOCOLATE, PEACH, OR CHERRY–CREAM CHEESE)

MAKES 8 HAND PIES

Hand pies were the original toaster pastries, as far as I'm concerned. I grew up eating these gems at county fairs and parties where their compact, portable shape made them easy to nibble while strolling outside during the sweltering Mississippi summers. Sometimes they were literally small versions of large pies that we'd eat sideways like pizza to keep the fillings from falling out of the crust. Other times they were folded turnovers like these, fried to a crisp golden brown and wrapped in brown butcher paper. Serve them at a picnic or as a to-go dessert after a long party.

Single batch (1 disk) Pastry Dough (page 81)

All-purpose flour for the work surface

Cherry-Cream Cheese Filling (recipe follows), Peach Cobbler Filling (recipe follows), or ¼ recipe Chocolate Cream Pie Filling (see page 74)

Egg wash (see page 80)

Vegetable oil for deep-frying

Place the dough on a floured work surface and cut into 8 equal pieces. Shape each piece into a flat disk and then return to the refrigerator to rest for 1 hour.

Working with one dough disk at a time, roll it out into a circle or square ¼ inch thick. Spoon one eighth of the filling onto the center of the circle or square, brush the edges with egg wash, then fold in half so the edges meet and enclose the filling in the center. If you're using a square dough, fold in half diagonally so that it forms a triangle. Using the tines of a fork, press around the seam to seal the edges tightly. Repeat to make 7 more pies and then refrigerate them all for 30 minutes. (The pies can be wrapped tightly in plastic at this point and frozen for up to 1 month.)

FRY THE HAND PIES: In a deep fryer or large cast-iron or enameled pot fitted with a deep-frying thermometer, heat about 3 inches of oil to 425°F. Add 4 of the pies and cook, turning frequently, until golden brown and the filling is piping hot, about 4 minutes. Using a slotted spoon or strainer, remove to a wire rack set over paper towels to drain. Fry the remaining pies, then serve when they're cool enough to handle but are still piping hot. Be careful: The fillings will scald the roof of your mouth worse than the tomato sauce on a slice of hot pizza.

## CHERRY-CREAM CHEESE FILLING

1 (8-ounce) package cream cheese, softened

2 tablespoons sugar

1 large egg

1 tablespoon kirsch (cherry brandy)

1 cup thawed or fresh pitted sour cherries

Put the cream cheese and sugar in a bowl and beat with a handheld mixer until smooth and fluffy. Add the egg and kirsch and beat until smooth. Stir in the cherries until evenly coated in cream cheese and refrigerate until ready to use.

## PEACH COBBLER FILLING

¼ cup sugar

1 tablespoon cornstarch

1 teaspoon fresh lemon juice

1 teaspoon Bourbon

½ teaspoon vanilla extract

¼ teaspoon kosher salt

Pinch each of ground cinnamon

Freshly grated nutmeg

1 pound peeled and pitted peaches, thawed if frozen, chopped or thinly sliced

Whisk together sugar, cornstarch, juice, Bourbon, vanilla, salt, cinnamon, and nutmeg. Add peaches and toss to coat.

## EGG WASH

Egg wash is a simple mixture of beaten egg with liquid; it might seem unnecessary, but the picture-perfect golden brown color it gives to baked goods is worth the small effort it takes. The protein in the egg white is what lends the browned surface its beautiful color, while the fat in the yolks keeps the outside of baked goods from drying too much. What liquid you mix with it affects the final outcome as well: Cream makes it richer, while oil results in a crisper finish. My all-purpose egg wash is a mixture of 1 large egg mixed with 1 tablespoon water and ½ teaspoon kosher salt. The salt darkens the proteins in the egg, giving an even richer color and imparting a slightly salty flavor as well, great even for sweet baked goods.

# PASTRY DOUGH

I use this pastry for everything, both sweet and savory. I usually double or triple this recipe and portion it out into disks that I can freeze and use for pie or tart making any time. This dough works like a dream and is a foolproof but impressive dough that's perfect for beginning pie makers.

1½ cups all-purpose flour

1½ teaspoons sugar

1 teaspoon kosher salt

½ cup (1 stick) cold unsalted butter, cut into cubes

¼ cup ice-cold water

In a bowl, combine the flour, sugar, and salt, then add the butter. Using your fingers, pinch the butter pieces into the flour until they form small pebbles. Make a well in the center of the flour and butter mixture and pour the ice water into it. Using a fork, bring the edges of the wall over the water and, spinning the bowl as you go, stir from the outside, constantly flinging flour from the outside wall into the center until all the flour is evenly moistened.

Dump the dough onto a clean work surface and push and knead it until the dough just begins to stick together. Form into a rough mound, then shape into a disk about 1 inch thick. If there are any cracks at the edge of the disk, press and smooth them out. Wrap in plastic wrap and refrigerate for at least 1 hour, or freeze for up to 1 month.

# Lemon Icebox Tart

Lemon icebox pie is one of those classic southern mainstays, right up there with pecan pie or banana pudding. I still remember fondly those slices I'd get from the church cafeteria, with the half-soggy vanilla wafers jutting out from the whipped cream on top of the icy, sour pie filling. Lemon juice here mingles with sweetened condensed milk, as in key lime pie, to set naturally (although I still bake mine with egg yolks just to be safe and get a clean, firm filling). It gets a generous covering of whipped cream, then chills in the fridge until you're ready to eat. I've updated it slightly here by shaping it into a tart, I hope persuading you to eat it out of hand while loitering around a picnic table on a hot summer day.

---

2 cups vanilla wafer crumbs (about 40 cookies, finely ground in a food processor)

½ cup sugar

½ cup (1 stick) unsalted butter, melted

2 cups fresh lemon juice

2 (14-ounce) cans sweetened condensed milk

2 large egg yolks

½ teaspoon kosher salt

1½ cups cold heavy cream

1 teaspoon vanilla extract

Heat the oven to 400°F.

In a food processor, process the cookie crumbs, sugar, and butter until evenly combined, then pour into an 11-inch tart pan with a removable bottom and press the mixture into the bottom and up the sides of the pan. In a bowl, combine the lemon juice, condensed milk, egg yolks, and salt and beat with a handheld mixer on medium-high speed for 5 minutes (this breaks down the proteins of the eggs and causes the chemical reaction between them and the lemon juice that will help set the filling). Pour over the crumb crust and bake until the filling is set but still slightly jiggly in the center, about 20 minutes. Let cool completely, then freeze until set, at least 2 hours or up to overnight.

When you're ready to serve the tart, whisk the cream and vanilla in a bowl until stiff peaks form. Transfer to a piping bag fitted with a ⅜-inch star tip and pipe the cream decoratively over the top of the tart. Refrigerate until ready to serve.

# Peanut Butter–Apple Tart

One of my favorite snacks as a kid was cut pieces of tart green apple with a big spoonful of peanut butter on top. Inspired by the combination, I decided to base this beautiful tart on it, one that transforms my humble childhood snack into a dessert that's as great for breakfast as it is after a big supper.

Single batch (1 disk) Pastry Dough (page 81)

12 ounces roasted salted peanuts (about 2⅓ cups)

3 tablespoons all-purpose flour

1½ cups packed light brown sugar

1 cup (2 sticks) unsalted butter

½ cup smooth peanut butter

2 large eggs

2 teaspoons vanilla extract

1 teaspoon kosher salt

2 tart green apples

2 teaspoons fresh lemon juice

Heat the oven to 375°F.

Roll the dough out to a round ¼ inch thick and line an 11-inch tart pan with a removable bottom with it; refrigerate until ready to use.

Put the peanuts in a food processor and process until very finely ground, about 1 minute. Add the flour, brown sugar, butter, peanut butter, eggs, vanilla, and salt and process until the mixture is a smooth paste, about another minute. (This is called a frangipane, basically a thick nut paste with just enough flour and eggs to thicken it into a firm base for fruit when baked.) Transfer the frangipane to the chilled pastry shell and spread it evenly in the bottom with an offset spatula or butter knife.

Peel, core, and roughly chop the apples into 1-inch cubes, then toss them with the lemon juice until evenly coated; distribute them evenly over the peanut frangipane. Gently press them into the frangipane with your hands, then bake until the crust is golden brown, the frangipane is thickened and browned, and the apples are slightly caramelized on their edges, about 45 minutes. Let the tart cool completely to allow the frangipane to set up, then serve at room temperature, cut into thin wedges, with a cold glass of milk.

# Lemon Meringue Pie

MAKES ONE 9-INCH DEEP-DISH PIE

This classic pie makes me philosophical about desserts. It's more than just ingredients mixed together and put to the heat to create an architectural wonder. It possesses the gold standard of pie fillings, a mixture able to bring forth memories of warming spring sunshine while drinking cooling lemonade and smelling fresh-cut grass. It's sweet simplicity at its finest. All this is just to say: This is a damn good pie.

Single batch (1 disk)
   Pastry Dough (page 81)

FOR THE FILLING:

1¼ cups sugar

6 tablespoons cornstarch

½ teaspoon kosher salt

1 cup milk

2 tablespoons grated lemon zest

¾ cup fresh lemon juice

6 large egg yolks

1½ tablespoons limoncello (optional; see Note)

2 tablespoons cold unsalted butter, cut into cubes

FOR THE MERINGUE:

1 cup sugar

4 large egg whites

1 teaspoon cornstarch

½ teaspoon cream of tartar

Heat the oven to 400°F. Roll the dough out to a round ¼ inch thick and line a 9-inch deep-dish pie pan with it, trimming the edges. Prick all over with the tines of a fork, line with parchment paper, and fill with pie weights or dried beans. Bake until the crust just begins to look tan and no longer raw, about 20 minutes. Remove the paper and weights and continue to bake until lightly browned and cooked through, about another 20 minutes. Let cool completely.

MAKE THE FILLING: In a medium-size saucepan, whisk together the sugar, cornstarch, and salt, then add the milk, ½ cup water, the lemon zest, lemon juice, and egg yolks. Whisking constantly, place over medium-high heat and bring to a boil; boil until thick and glossy, 2 to 3 minutes. Stir in the limoncello (if using) and remove from the heat. Add the butter and whisk until it's melted into the filling. Pour the filling through a sieve into the cooled piecrust.

MAKE THE MERINGUE: Put the sugar and ½ cup water in a small saucepan with a candy thermometer attached to the side of the pan and bring to a boil. In the bowl of a stand mixer fitted with the whisk attachment, combine the egg whites, cornstarch, and cream of tartar and beat on medium speed until soft peaks form. Cook the syrup until it reaches 240°F, then slowly pour it into the beating egg whites. Continue beating until glossy, stiff peaks form and the meringue is just warm to the touch. Immediately cover the pie with the meringue, creating swirls and peaks with a rubber spatula, then use a blowtorch to brown the top (see page 44). Let cool to room temperature, then refrigerate until chilled.

NOTE: While not essential in this pie, limoncello, a relatively inexpensive liqueur often served as an after-dinner digestif in Italy, is a great ingredient to further bolster the lemon flavor. But if you don't have it, don't worry: This pie will still taste wonderful without it.

# Peach Cobbler

## SERVES 12 TO 16

When it comes to baked fruit desserts, the names can get a little silly and very confusing: Crumbles, buckles, grunts, slumps, and brown Bettys—they're all different, but only very slightly. By most definitions, a cobbler is a baked fruit filling topped with biscuit dumplings, but every version I ever had growing up was topped with a piecrust, either latticed or whole. Peaches are classic, but you can use virtually any fruit in this cobbler and the dessert will come out spectacularly. Whenever I make pie dough, I freeze any leftover scraps to reuse as cobbler topping. The scraps' jagged texture creates a perfect crunchy contrast to the bubbly fruit filling. My thrifty southern grandparents would be so proud.

---

1 cup sugar, plus more for sprinkling on top

¼ cup cornstarch

1 tablespoon fresh lemon juice

1 tablespoon Bourbon

2 teaspoons vanilla extract

1 teaspoon kosher salt

½ teaspoon ground cinnamon

¼ teaspoon freshly grated nutmeg

4 pounds peeled and pitted peaches, thawed if frozen, chopped or thinly sliced

Single batch (1 disk) Pastry Dough (page 81), rolled out ¼ inch thick and cut into strips 1½ inches wide, then frozen; or 1 pound frozen leftover scraps of pastry dough

¼ cup (½ stick) unsalted butter, cut into cubes

Vanilla Soft-Serve (page 206)

Heat the oven to 375°F.

In a large bowl, whisk together the 1 cup sugar and the cornstarch, then add the lemon juice, Bourbon, vanilla, salt, cinnamon, and nutmeg and stir until evenly combined. Add the peaches and toss until evenly coated in the spiced sugar. Transfer to a 3-quart baking dish and spread evenly in the bottom.

Break the frozen strips of pastry into jagged pieces and distribute them evenly over the peaches. Top with the cubes of butter, then sprinkle liberally with more sugar. Bake until the peaches are bubbling in the center and the pastry is deep golden brown, about 1 hour 15 minutes. Let cool for about 15 minutes before serving with large scoops of soft-serve.

# Peanut Butter Pie

MAKES ONE 9-INCH PIE

My mom used to make this pie all the time for picnics when I was growing up. Hers consisted mostly of vanilla pudding and whipped cream, with only a small amount of peanut butter stirred into confectioners' sugar. It still tasted like heaven, but when I made my version, I wanted to showcase the peanut butter itself, so I use brown sugar to add even more warm, nutty butterscotch flavor.

Single batch (1 disk) Pastry Dough (page 81)

1 cup confectioners' sugar

1 cup smooth peanut butter

½ cup packed light brown sugar

¼ cup cornstarch

1 teaspoon kosher salt

5 large egg yolks

2 cups milk

2 tablespoons unsalted butter, cut into cubes

1 tablespoon plus 1 teaspoon vanilla extract

1 cup heavy cream

2 tablespoons granulated sugar

Heat the oven to 425°F.

Roll the dough out to a round ¼ inch thick and line a 9-inch pie pan with it, trimming the edges. Prick all over with the tines of a fork, line with parchment paper, and fill with pie weights or dried beans. Bake for 20 minutes, then remove the paper and weights and continue to cook until golden brown, about 12 minutes more. Let cool completely.

In a bowl, stir together the confectioners' sugar and ½ cup of the peanut butter with a fork until it forms crumbles (you'll see what I mean when it gets there); reserve ½ cup of the crumbles and refrigerate until ready to use. Spread the remaining crumbles in the bottom of the cooled crust. In a medium-size saucepan, whisk together the brown sugar, cornstarch, and salt, then add the egg yolks, stirring until smooth. Whisk in the milk until smooth, then bring to a simmer over medium heat. Cook the custard, whisking constantly, until it thickens to the consistency of loose pudding, then continue to cook for another minute. Remove from the heat and whisk in the remaining ½ cup peanut butter until smooth. Add the butter and 1 tablespoon of the vanilla and whisk until smooth and emulsified. Pour the custard over the crumbles in the pie shell and smooth the top with a rubber spatula. Refrigerate until well chilled and set, at least 4 hours or up to overnight.

When ready to serve, whisk together the remaining 1 teaspoon vanilla, the cream, and granulated sugar until stiff peaks form, then spread evenly over the pie, creating peaks and valleys in the cream with your spatula. Sprinkle the reserved crumbles on top of the whipped cream, letting them fall into the valleys. Serve chilled.

# Pecan Pie

My mom made her pecan pie virtually every week while I was growing up, and to this day it still gets rave reviews. The secret? Well, there are a few: Browned butter mirrors the intense flavor of the toasted pecans. Lots of lemon juice cuts through the sweetness of the filling. Last, the pie is completely packed with pecans, by which I mean it's practically brimming with nuts, with just enough custardy filling to hold it all together. Mom used Karo corn syrup, as do most people still, but I've found that my homemade version (see below) works even better.

Single batch (1 disk) Pastry Dough (page 81)

½ cup (1 stick) unsalted butter

1 cup sugar

1 cup homemade "corn syrup" (recipe follows)

4 large eggs

1 tablespoon fresh lemon juice

1 teaspoon vanilla extract

½ teaspoon kosher salt

2 cups roughly chopped pecans

Heat the oven to 375°F.

Roll the dough out to a round ¼ inch thick and line a 9-inch deep-dish pie pan with it. Place the pie pan on a parchment paper–lined baking sheet and refrigerate until ready to use.

Put the butter in a medium-size saucepan and cook over medium heat, stirring occasionally, until it begins to brown and smell nutty. Remove from the heat and stir in the sugar and corn syrup, stirring until smooth (the sugar doesn't need to be completely dissolved). Add the eggs, lemon juice, vanilla, and salt and whisk until smooth. Add the pecans and stir until evenly combined. Pour into the chilled pastry shell (the filling will come almost to the top of the crust) and carefully transfer to the oven. Bake for 10 minutes, then lower the oven temperature to 325°F and continue to bake until the custard is set and the pecans and crust are deep golden brown, 45 to 50 minutes more. Let the pie cool completely before slicing and serving.

## Good to Know: HOMEMADE "CORN SYRUP"

In a small saucepan, bring 2 cups sugar, ½ cup water, and 2 teaspoons fresh lemon juice just to a boil, swirling the pan until the sugar dissolves. Brush the edges of the pan with a wet pastry brush to prevent crystals from forming. Remove from the heat and let cool. Essentially an acidified, thickened simple syrup, this can also be made with light brown sugar, turbinado sugar, or other granulated sweeteners.

# Pecan-Cranberry Linzer Torte

MAKES ONE 9-INCH TART

Linzer torte has always been one of my favorite "underdog" desserts. It's an old-school classic that few people make anymore. Instead of the traditional hazelnuts, I use my favorite nut, pecans. Cranberry preserves lend a pleasing tartness that makes this dessert a welcome addition to the Thanksgiving table. I get around the fragility of the dough by pressing the bottom layer into the tart pan instead of rolling it out. I freeze the dough strips for the latticed top on parchment paper. This makes them infinitely easier to work with and keeps the top looking as crisp and beautiful as the Viennese pastry shop version.

---

⅔ cup packed light brown sugar

½ cup (1 stick) unsalted butter, at room temperature

1 large egg

2 cups all-purpose flour, plus more for the work surface

½ cup ground toasted pecans (3 ounces)

¾ teaspoon ground cinnamon

½ teaspoon baking powder

½ teaspoon salt

2 cups natural cranberry preserves, chunky or smooth (see page 68)

In a bowl, combine the brown sugar and butter and beat with a handheld mixer on medium-high speed until lightened in color and fluffy, about 4 minutes. Add the egg and beat until smooth. In another bowl, whisk together the flour, pecans, cinnamon, baking powder, and salt, then add to the butter mixture and beat on low speed until just combined and smooth. Transfer the dough to a lightly floured work surface, quickly form into a rough ball, and divide the ball almost in half, with one piece slightly larger than the other. Place the smaller dough piece on a sheet of parchment paper, cover with another sheet, and refrigerate for 1 hour. Place the larger dough piece in a 9-inch tart pan with a removable bottom and break apart into small chunks. Spread the chunks around the bottom of the tart pan. Gently begin pressing the chunks flat to form a crust covering the bottom and up the side of the tart pan. Refrigerate the tart pan for 1 hour.

Remove the smaller dough piece covered in parchment and transfer it to a work surface. Using a rolling pin, roll the ball in the parchment into a roughly 10-inch square. Transfer to a baking sheet and freeze the dough in parchment for 30 minutes. Using a sharp knife or pizza cutter, cut the chilled sheet of dough, still between the parchment sheets, into 1-inch-wide strips. Peel away the parchment paper from the top, flip the strips on the bottom parchment over onto a clean sheet of parchment, then peel away the top parchment again so you have the cut strips of dough exposed on top of a clean sheet of parchment. Return to the freezer.

Heat the preserves in a small saucepan until loosened, then pour over the chilled crust in the tart pan. Working quickly, arrange 4 or 5 frozen strips of dough parallel over the preserves, then lay the remaining 4 or 5 strips perpendicular, or at a 45-degree angle, over the first strips. Let sit for 5 minutes to allow the dough strips to soften slightly, then press them into the edges of the bottom crust to trim them flush with the tart pan and also adhere them to the bottom crust dough.

Heat the oven to 375°F.

Bake the tart until the preserves are bubbling in the center and the dough is cooked through and darkened, about 30 minutes. Let cool completely before serving.

# Persimmon Pie

MAKES ONE 9-INCH DEEP-DISH PIE

Since moving to California a couple years back, I've been inundated with persimmons. Fuyus and Hachiyas were practically falling into the streets when I first arrived, and after growing up with the fruit in Mississippi, I was like a kid in a candy store. My favorites are the Fuyus, those that look like squat orange tomatoes. This pie, a spin on a classic double-crust apple pie, is my favorite way to use them. Like apples, the persimmon slices break down into a supple, sweet filling but don't lose their structure. A giant scoop of Vanilla Soft-Serve (page 206) or Spice Ice Cream (page 205) is all you need to finish off this beauty.

Double recipe (2 disks) Pastry Dough (page 81)

3 pounds Fuyu persimmons, cored, halved crosswise, seeded, and cut into ¼-inch-thick slices

½ cup plus 1 tablespoon sugar

½ cup cornstarch

1 tablespoon grated orange zest

2 tablespoons fresh orange juice

1 vanilla bean, seeds scraped

1 teaspoon ground cardamom

1 teaspoon kosher salt

2 tablespoons heavy cream

Roll one dough disk out to a round ¼ inch thick and line a 9-inch deep-dish pie pan with it. Roll the other disk out to a round ¼ inch thick and place it on a parchment paper–lined baking sheet; refrigerate both until ready to use.

Heat the oven to 425°F.

In a large bowl, whisk together the ½ cup sugar and the cornstarch until evenly combined, then whisk in the orange zest, orange juice, vanilla bean seeds, cardamom, and salt until evenly combined. Add the persimmons and toss until evenly coated in the spiced sugar. Pour the persimmons into the pie pan and spread them evenly in the bottom, piling them into a mound in the center, if necessary. Brush the edge of the dough with water, then transfer the dough round to the pie on top of the persimmons, pressing it onto the bottom crust at the edge. Trim the crusts so they have 1 inch of overhang, then fold the overhang under itself and rest it on the edge of the pie plate; crimp with a fork or your fingers to seal and press the top and bottom crusts together at the edge. Cut a hole in the center of the top, then brush all the exposed dough with the cream and sprinkle with the remaining 1 tablespoon sugar. Bake until the crust is golden brown and the filling is bubbling in the center, about 1 hour 10 minutes. Let cool completely before slicing and serving.

# Pineapple Tarte Tatin

How can you improve on a classic as beloved and delicious as pineapple upside-down cake? Make it crispier! Pineapple upside-down cake is a wonder, but if you're ever in the mood for a slimmer, more crunch-filled version, I implore you to make this tart: thick slices of pineapple, crisp buttery crust, and just enough caramel to glue them together. It's a simple update on the original with every bit as much appeal.

---

¾ cup (1½ sticks) unsalted butter

½ cup packed light brown sugar

2 tablespoons rum

1 teaspoon vanilla extract

7 (½-inch-thick) crosswise slices fresh pineapple, cored

½ cup fresh or frozen pitted sour cherries

1 (14-ounce) package frozen puff pastry, thawed

Vanilla Soft-Serve (page 206) for serving

Heat the oven to 400°F.

Melt the butter in a 12-inch nonstick skillet over medium-high heat. Whisk in the brown sugar, rum, and vanilla until the sugar is dissolved, then remove the skillet from the heat. Arrange the pineapple slices in the bottom of the skillet, then arrange the cherries evenly in and among the pineapple slices.

Unfold the puff pastry sheet and cut it into a circle, about 10 inches in diameter, and fit it over the fruit, tucking the edges down the side of the skillet to completely cover the fruit. Prick the pastry all over with the tines of a fork and bake until the pastry is puffed and golden brown and caramel is bubbling around the edge of the skillet, about 30 minutes. Transfer the skillet to a wire rack and let cool for 2 minutes. Place a large plate or serving platter upside down over the skillet and, using pot holders or towels, carefully and quickly invert the plate and skillet together, letting the tarte tatin fall onto the plate. It should all fall together, but if some of the fruit sticks to the pan, simply rearrange it over the crust while no one's looking.

Cut into wedges and serve with large scoops of soft-serve, which melts and pools perfectly in the crevices of the pineapple and pastry.

# Pumpkin Kanafe

MAKES ONE 9-INCH PIE

During my time in New York City, I lived in Astoria, Queens, one of the planet's most ethnically diverse zip code and home to large, well-established Greek and Middle Eastern communities. In one strip of the neighborhood, affectionately called Little Cairo, there was a sweets shop that made *kanafe*, a traditional pastry of shredded phyllo filled with sweet cheese, baked, and drenched in a spiced syrup. That syrup reminded me of all the flavors of pumpkin pie minus the pumpkin. For my rendition here, I fill it with pumpkin and cream cheese, and drench it in a fragrant syrup of cinnamon, cloves, allspice, and orange.

1 cup sugar

1 teaspoon kosher salt

8 whole cloves

1 nutmeg pod, crushed

3 cinnamon sticks

4 allspice berries

½ orange, cut crosswise into ¼-inch-thick slices

10 ounces frozen shredded phyllo dough (called *kataifi*; see Note), defrosted and roughly chopped

1 cup (2 sticks) unsalted butter, melted

1 pound cooked and pureed pumpkin (canned or fresh)

4 ounces cream cheese, softened

Sour cream for garnish

3 tablespoons ground toasted pecans for garnish

In a small saucepan, combine the sugar, salt, cloves, nutmeg, cinnamon sticks, allspice, orange, and ¾ cup water. Bring to a boil and cook, stirring, until the sugar is dissolved and the syrup is fragrant, about 5 minutes. Remove from the heat and let cool while you make the *kanafe*.

Heat the oven to 375°F.

Combine the phyllo dough and ¾ cup of the melted butter in a food processor and pulse until just combined, about 30 seconds. Grease a 9-inch pie pan with 2 tablespoons of the remaining butter, then transfer half of the phyllo to the pan and flatten it evenly over the bottom. Stir together the pumpkin and cream cheese until smooth, then spread it evenly over the phyllo. Cover with the remaining phyllo and flatten it into an even layer. Drizzle the top with the remaining 2 tablespoons butter, then bake until golden brown, about 1 hour. Right before the *kanafe* comes out of the oven, pour the spiced syrup through a sieve into a bowl and discard the spices.

Transfer the *kanafe* in the pie pan to a wire rack and slowly drizzle the top and sides with the syrup. Let the *kanafe* sit to allow the syrup time to soak into the *kanafe*, about 5 minutes, then slice the *kanafe* into large wedges and serve topped with dollops of sour cream and sprinkled with the pecans.

NOTE: *Kataifi* is finely shredded phyllo dough, used to lend a crunchy, haystack-like texture to pastries. Usually sold frozen in Middle Eastern grocery stores or ethnic markets, it can also be baked on its own and crumbled on top of fruit desserts or used as a coating for breaded-and-fried foods.

# Shaker Key Lime Pie

MAKES ONE 9-INCH DEEP-DISH PIE

Shaker lemon pie is wonderful, but I've always wondered how lime's bracingly tart, slightly bitter flavor would fare in it. This variation was born one summer out of an abundance of Key limes, the smaller, milder cousins of Persian limes. I slice them thinly and toss them into a filling for this pie. Their tart yet brighter-than-lemon quality goes so well with all the sugar needed for this pie. I also make the filling with regular limes since those are easier to get and just as good. But if you happen to get your hands on Key limes, by all means use them here and you'll never go back to lemon. Be sure to start the pie well in advance, as the limes need to macerate in the sugar for 24 hours.

---

12 ounces Key limes,
  or 6 regular limes (pictured)

2 cups sugar

1 teaspoon kosher salt

4 large eggs

4 tablespoons (½ stick)
  unsalted butter, melted

3 tablespoons all-purpose
  flour

Single batch (1 disk) Pastry
  Dough (page 81)

Finely grate the zest from the limes into a bowl. Using a mandoline or a sharp knife, thinly slice the limes and discard the seeds. Add the lime slices to the zest, along with the sugar and salt. Toss together evenly, then cover and set aside at room temperature for 24 hours.

Roll the dough out into a round ¼ inch thick and line a 9-inch deep-dish pie pan with it, trimming the edges; refrigerate until ready to use.

Heat the oven to 375°F.

Whisk the eggs in a large bowl until smooth and loosened, then add the butter and flour and whisk until smooth. Add the lime and sugar mixture and stir until evenly combined. Pour into the chilled pastry shell and evenly distribute the lime slices. Bake until the crust and filling are golden brown and the filling is set but still barely loose in the middle, 45 to 50 minutes. Let cool completely before slicing and serving.

# Treacle Cashew Tart

British desserts are some of my very favorites, and treacle tart tops that list, with its undiluted filling made with Lyle's golden syrup. It's like pecan pie, but without nuts. Here, I add rich, salty cashews to the custard filling, which creates a fantastically decadent dessert that tastes like the most amazing caramel-nut candy bar you've ever had.

---

Single batch (1 disk) Pastry Dough (page 81)

1 cup Lyle's golden syrup

½ cup heavy cream

2 large eggs, lightly beaten

2 tablespoons leftover yellow cake crumbs or plain bread crumbs (see Note)

1½ cups salted cashews

Heat the oven to 375°F.

Roll the dough out into a round ¼ inch thick and line a 9-inch tart pan with a removable bottom with it; refrigerate until ready to use.

Put the syrup in a small saucepan and heat over medium heat until loosened, about 5 minutes. Remove from the heat and stir in the cream. Add the eggs and crumbs and whisk until smooth. Add the cashews and stir until evenly coated. Pour into the pastry shell and evenly distribute the cashews. Bake until the filling and crust are golden brown and the filling is set, about 30 minutes. Let cool completely before serving.

NOTE: Recipes for treacle tart typically call for bread crumbs as a binder in the filling, and indeed plain (unseasoned) bread crumbs will work just fine here. I prefer to use cake crumbs, though, because to me they're a more natural fit for the filling. If you have any leftover yellow or vanilla cake (see page 121), crumble it finely and use it here.

# Triple Cherry Pie

MAKES ONE 9-INCH DEEP-DISH PIE

When putting the spotlight on one simple ingredient in a recipe—as in the cherries here—I try to incorporate it in as many ways, shapes, and forms as possible. For this classic pie, I boost the flavor of tart summer cherries with tangy cherry preserves and with kirsch, an elegant cherry brandy that is, hands down, my favorite spirit.

Double recipe (2 disks) Pastry Dough (page 81)

⅔ cup cherry preserves (see page 68)

½ cup cornstarch

¼ cup plus 1 tablespoon sugar

2 tablespoons fresh lemon juice

1 tablespoon kirsch (cherry brandy)

2 teaspoons vanilla extract

1 teaspoon kosher salt

¼ teaspoon freshly grated nutmeg

2 pounds pitted whole fresh or thawed frozen sour cherries

4 tablespoons (½ stick) unsalted butter, cut into cubes

1 large egg, lightly beaten

Roll one dough disk out to a round ¼ inch thick and line a 9-inch deep-dish pie pan with it. Roll the other disk out to a round ¼ inch thick and place it on a parchment paper–lined baking sheet; refrigerate both until ready to use.

Heat the oven to 375°F.

In a large bowl, whisk together the preserves, cornstarch, and ¼ cup of the sugar until evenly combined, then whisk in the lemon juice, kirsch, vanilla, salt, and nutmeg until evenly combined. Add the cherries and toss until evenly coated in the spiced preserves. Pour the cherries into the pastry shell and spread them evenly in the bottom, piling them into a mound in the center, if necessary. Brush the edge of the pastry with water, then transfer the dough round to the top of the cherries, pressing it onto the bottom crust at the edge. Trim the crusts so they have 1 inch of overhang, then fold the overhang under itself and rest it on the edge of the pie pan; crimp with a fork or your fingers to seal and press the bottom and top crusts together at the edge. Cut a hole in the center of the top crust, then brush the exposed dough with beaten egg and sprinkle with the remaining 1 tablespoon sugar. Bake until the crust is golden brown and the filling is bubbling in the center, about 1 hour 25 minutes. Let cool completely before slicing and serving.

# Biscuits, Breads & Pastries

BANANA BISCUIT DUMPLINGS IN SYRUP

BANANA BREAD

CANE SYRUP AND SPICE MUFFINS

CARDAMOM "ÉCLAIRS"

CLASSIC GLAZED DOUGHNUTS

CLASSIC SOUTHERN BISCUITS

CORN BREAD PUDDING WITH WHISKEY CARAMEL SAUCE

PECAN AND SYRUP PANCAKE STACK

CREAM CHEESE–LAYERED CINNAMON ROLLS

EDAM CHEESE ROLLS

GERMAN SUGAR BREAD

ORANGE BREAKFAST ROLLS

NEW ORLEANS KING CAKE

PEACH MELBA SUMMER PUDDING

STRAWBERRY GRUNT

# Banana Biscuit Dumplings in Syrup

SERVES 8

I give this traditional French-Canadian dessert called "grand-père" a southern twist by flavoring the biscuits with spicy cinnamon and sweet chopped bananas and steaming them in my own homemade pancake syrup (pure Grade A maple syrup is delicious, too). The tender dumplings, suffused with warm syrup, always remind me of that perfect last bite of any plate of pancakes, where the syrup has completely soaked through the fluffy cake.

1¾ cups all-purpose flour

5 teaspoons baking powder

½ teaspoon ground cinnamon

1 teaspoon kosher salt

4 tablespoons (½ stick) unsalted butter, frozen

¾ cup buttermilk

1 overripe banana, peeled and mashed

2 cups pancake syrup, homemade (page 120) or store-bought

In a large bowl, combine the flour, baking powder, cinnamon, and salt and whisk until combined. Using a cheese grater, grate the butter into the dry ingredients and stir until all the butter pieces are coated in flour. Pour in the buttermilk and mashed banana and stir until a dough forms. Refrigerate the dough for at least 30 minutes.

Put the syrup and 1½ cups water in a large, heavy saucepan with a lid. Bring to a steady simmer, then remove the dough from the refrigerator and, using a large soupspoon, drop balls of dough into the syrup, spacing them evenly apart as you drop them. Cover the pan and cook the dumplings until tender and cooked through, 10 to 15 minutes.

Serve the dumplings in bowls, drenched with syrup from the pan.

# Banana Bread

My mom made this banana bread all the time as a snack or for breakfast before church on Sundays. It's more akin to a banana muffin batter, and when it bakes up it has the texture of a fudgy brownie. People who, like me, prefer their banana bread so moist and dense as to be almost fudgy will—forgive me—go bananas for this intense variation on the classic recipe. Wrapped in plastic wrap, this bread will stay moist for days, although none has ever lasted that long in our house. It's ridiculously over the top, and that's how I like it.

2 cups all-purpose flour

1½ teaspoons baking soda

1 teaspoon kosher salt

1½ cups roughly chopped pecans

2 cups sugar

1 cup canola oil

⅔ cup buttermilk

2 large whole eggs

2 large egg yolks

2 teaspoons vanilla extract

6 very ripe bananas, peeled and mashed

Heat the oven to 350°F. Spray two 9-by-5-inch loaf pans evenly with baking spray.

In a large bowl, whisk together the flour, baking soda, and salt, then stir in the pecans. In another bowl, whisk together the sugar, oil, buttermilk, whole eggs and egg yolks, and vanilla until smooth, then add the bananas and stir until smooth. Pour the wet ingredients over the dry ingredients and whisk until evenly combined and smooth. Divide the batter between the prepared pans and bake, rotating the pans halfway through, until a toothpick inserted in the middle of each comes out clean, about 1 hour 15 minutes.

Let the cakes cool in the pans for about 20 minutes, then invert onto wire racks and let cool completely before serving.

# Cane Syrup and Spice Muffins

MAKES 12 MUFFINS

These are just the kind of muffins you want on a really cold winter morning. Granted, we may not get many of those down South, but we learned to appreciate the virtues of a delicious, comforting muffin just the same. Steen's cane syrup, still manufactured in Abbeville, Louisiana, is known across the South and lends these muffins a deep sweetness that complements warm spices like cinnamon, ginger, and cloves.

1½ cups all-purpose flour

2 teaspoons baking powder

1 teaspoon ground cinnamon

1 teaspoon ground ginger

¼ teaspoon ground cloves

½ teaspoon kosher salt

1 cup Steen's dark cane syrup,
   Lyle's golden syrup, or maple syrup

½ cup freshly squeezed orange juice

¼ cup vegetable or canola oil

1 large egg, beaten

Heat the oven to 350°F. Spray a 12-cup muffin pan with baking spray.

In a large bowl, combine the flour, baking powder, cinnamon, ginger, cloves, and salt and whisk until evenly combined. In a glass measuring cup, combine the syrup, orange juice, oil, and egg and whisk until smooth. Pour the wet ingredients over the dry ingredients and whisk until just combined. Using a 2-ounce ice cream scoop or ¼-cup measuring cup, spoon ¼ cup batter into each muffin cup. Bake until a toothpick inserted in the middle comes out clean, 20 to 25 minutes. Let cool in the pan for 10 minutes, then invert the muffins onto a wire rack. Let cool completely before serving.

## Good to Know: LYLE'S GOLDEN SYRUP

Known as treacle in the United Kingdom, golden syrup, made exclusively by Tate & Lyle's, is a staple of the British pantry, much like corn syrup or maple syrup in the United States. The rich butterscotch flavor of treacle is so wonderful it got its own tart. While it is not a direct substitution for the afore-mentioned American syrups because of its thickness, I like to use it in places where I would normally use another syrup, drizzled on pancakes, cooked in fudge, as a sweetener for tea, or as a filling for pie. My Treacle Cashew Tart (page 104) uses it much like you would in a treacle tart or pecan pie: to both sweeten and thicken the filling. It mimics the stewed figs' syrupy sweetness in the Fig Tart (page 76) and its complex flavor adds dimension to my tangy, salty Buttermilk Caramels (page 184). It's available stateside, but only in better supermarkets and specialty shops. It's also available online at Amazon.com, and it lasts, supposedly, forever; so if you do order a couple of tins online, you'll have years to think of amazing ways to use it and incorporate it into your own baking recipes.

# Cardamom "Éclairs"

## MAKES 16 PASTRIES

I first discovered these while developing a recipe to show off the warm perfume of cardamom. A traditional Lenten treat in Sweden, the hollowed bread rolls would be filled with almond paste and doused with warm milk. I took this as a jumping-off point and used a thick, rich cardamom-infused cream instead. Transforming the buns into elegant éclairs makes them easier to eat and keeps the cream filling from gushing out the sides.

FOR THE FILLING:

½ cup sugar

2 tablespoons cornstarch

1 tablespoon ground cardamom

½ teaspoon kosher salt

1 cup milk

2 large eggs

4 tablespoons (½ stick) unsalted butter, cut into cubes

⅔ cup heavy cream

1 teaspoon vanilla extract

FOR THE DOUGH:

½ cup milk heated to 115°F

¼ cup sugar

1 teaspoon ground cardamom

1 (¼-ounce) package active dry yeast

1 large egg yolk

2 cups all-purpose flour

1½ teaspoons baking powder

½ teaspoon kosher salt

3 tablespoons unsalted butter, cut into cubes, softened

Egg wash (see page 80)

Confectioners' sugar

MAKE THE FILLING: In a small saucepan, whisk together the sugar, cornstarch, cardamom, and salt, then whisk in the milk and eggs. Bring to a boil over medium heat and cook, whisking constantly, until thickened to the consistency of stiff pudding, about 1 minute. Remove from the heat and whisk in the butter. Transfer the mixture to a bowl and press a piece of plastic wrap onto its surface to prevent a skin from forming. Let this pastry cream cool completely to room temperature. In a bowl, whisk the cream and vanilla to semistiff peaks, then fold it gently into the pastry cream. Transfer the filling to a piping bag fitted with a plain or fluted tip and refrigerate until ready to use.

MAKE THE DOUGH: In the bowl of a stand mixer fitted with the paddle attachment, combine the milk, sugar, cardamom, and yeast. Stir together, then let sit until foamy, about 10 minutes. Stir in the egg yolk, then add the flour, baking powder, and salt and mix with the paddle until a dough forms. Replace the paddle with the dough hook attachment, add the butter, and knead on medium speed until the butter is incorporated and the dough is smooth and elastic, about 8 minutes. Remove the bowl from the mixer, cover with plastic wrap, and let the dough sit until doubled in size, about 1 hour.

Heat the oven to 400°F.

Transfer the dough to a work surface and divide into 16 equal portions. Roll each portion into a 4-inch-long finger-shaped log and place 8 logs each on two parchment paper-lined baking sheets; cover both baking sheets loosely with plastic wrap and let sit until the dough has risen slightly, about 30 minutes. Uncover and brush each dough log with egg wash, then bake, rotating the baking sheets halfway through, until golden brown, 18 to 20 minutes. Transfer to a wire rack and let cool completely.

Using a knife, cut off the top third of each bun or split the buns in half horizontally like a submarine sandwich, whatever you prefer. Pull out most of the dough from the inside of each bun. (Save it for bread crumbs or the Treacle Cashew Tart [page 104].) Pipe chilled cardamom cream into each log and cover with its top. Dust the filled logs with confectioners' sugar right before serving.

# Classic Glazed Doughnuts

Why make your own doughnuts? Well, I know that if I went into a Krispy Kreme, which are everywhere across the South, every time I saw the "Hot Donuts" sign lit in the window, my friends would never hear from me again. This recipe enables you to keep your friends!

---

FOR THE DOUGHNUTS:

1 tablespoon active dry yeast

6 tablespoons sugar

½ cup slightly warm water

1 cup buttermilk

2 large egg whites, lightly beaten

4½ cups all-purpose flour, plus more for the work surface

1½ teaspoons kosher salt

6 tablespoons (¾ stick) unsalted butter, cut into cubes, at room temperature

Canola oil for greasing and frying

FOR THE GLAZE:

3 cups confectioners' sugar

6 tablespoons heavy cream

1 tablespoon vanilla extract

The night before you plan to fry the doughnuts, make the dough: Stir together the yeast, a large pinch of the sugar, and the water in the bowl of a stand mixer fitted with the dough hook. Let sit for about 10 minutes, until foamy. Add the remaining sugar, the buttermilk, and egg whites and stir until evenly combined. Add the flour and salt and mix on medium speed until the dough comes together and is smooth, about 2 minutes. Add the butter and continue kneading until the butter is incorporated into the dough and the dough is smooth, about 6 minutes more. Cover the bowl with plastic wrap and let sit until the dough has doubled in size, about 2 hours. Meanwhile, line two large baking sheets with parchment paper and brush the paper with oil to grease liberally.

Transfer the dough to a lightly floured work surface and, using a floured rolling pin, roll the dough out to about ½ inch thick. Using a 4-inch round cutter, cut out rounds of dough, then cut out their centers using a 1½-inch round cutter. Transfer the dough rings and centers to the prepared baking sheets and reroll the scraps once to cut out more dough rings and centers. Transfer the baking sheets to the refrigerator and let the dough rings and centers rise in the refrigerator overnight, at least 8 hours and up to 12 hours.

The next morning, remove the dough rings and centers from the refrigerator and let sit at room temperature for 1 hour. Heat about 3 inches of oil to 425°F in a deep-fryer or large cast-iron or enameled pot fitted with a deep-frying thermometer. Working in batches, add the dough rings and fry until golden brown on the bottom, about 2 minutes. Flip the doughnuts and fry until golden brown all over and cooked through, 1 to 2 minutes more. Using tongs, lift the doughnuts from the oil and transfer to a wire rack set over paper towels to drain. When all the rings have been fried, add the centers to the oil and fry, turning in the oil until golden brown all over, about 2 minutes. Drain on a wire rack and let cool until easy to handle.

MAKE THE GLAZE: In a small saucepan, whisk together the confectioners' sugar, cream, and vanilla until smooth. Heat over low heat until warm and the sugar is completely dissolved. One at a time, place the doughnuts in the glaze, flip to coat, then return to the rack to drain and let the glaze set before serving.

# Classic Southern Biscuits

(WITH APPLE BUTTER, HOMEMADE PANCAKE SYRUP, AND STRAWBERRY-TOMATO-PEPPER JAM)

MAKES ABOUT 20 BISCUITS

If there's one recipe I cherish more than any other, it's this one. My grandmother Carol passed this recipe to my mother, who'd make them for me on Saturday mornings, topped with a generous pat of butter then doused with plenty of Blackburn's syrup. My philosophy is that no biscuit should be eaten more than ten minutes from the oven: Serve these piping hot.

---

4 cups all-purpose flour, plus more for the work surface

3 tablespoons baking powder

1 teaspoon baking soda

1 teaspoon kosher salt

1½ cups (3 sticks) cold unsalted butter, cut into ½-inch cubes

1½ cups cold buttermilk

FOR SERVING (OPTIONAL):

Butter

Apple Butter (page 120)

Homemade Pancake Syrup (page 120)

Strawberry-Tomato-Pepper Jam (page 121)

Line a baking sheet with parchment paper.

In a large bowl, whisk together the flour, baking powder, baking soda, and salt. Add the butter and, using your fingers, rub and crush the butter cubes into the flour, over and over again, until they resemble small crumbles with a few larger pieces of butter remaining. Form a well in the flour with your hands, then pour in the buttermilk. Using a fork, slowly bring in the flour from the side of the bowl and stir until a shaggy, wet dough begins forming. Once you see no loose pools of buttermilk in the bowl while stirring, dump the dough out onto a floured work surface and pat into a 1-inch-thick round. Using well-floured hands, start at one side and roll the sheet of dough like a jelly roll and arrange it seam side down. Flatten it again with your hands into about a 1-inch-thick round. Using a 2¾-inch round cutter (or another size, depending on how big or small you like your biscuits), cut out rounds and place them on the prepared baking sheet, spaced about 1 inch apart. Freeze until firm, at least 1 hour or overnight and up to 1 week. Reroll the scraps to make more biscuits, but know that those will be slightly less tender due to the extra rolling.

When ready to serve, heat the oven to 425°F.

Place the baking sheet with the biscuits, directly from the freezer, into the oven and bake until lightly golden brown and risen, 20 to 25 minutes. Serve the biscuits piping hot from the oven, allowing everyone to "ooh" and "ahh" over burning their fingers while handling them, spreading them with butter and apple butter, syrup, or jam while steam still rises from their insides.

# APPLE BUTTER

MAKES ABOUT 3 CUPS

If you want a deeper, more caramelized flavor, simply continue cooking the apple butter once it starts sticking to the pan, stirring often so it doesn't burn, until you reach your desired level of caramelization. But once it turns as dark as an amber caramel, remove it from the heat or it will burn.

2 pounds tart apples, such as Granny Smith or Fuji, peeled, cored, and roughly chopped

1¼ cups sugar

⅓ cup fresh lemon juice

1 spent vanilla bean

1 teaspoon kosher salt

In a medium-size saucepan, combine the apples, sugar, lemon juice, vanilla bean, and salt and stir until evenly combined. Let sit for about 10 minutes to allow the sugar to pull some juices from the apples. Place the pan over medium-low heat and cover the pan. Cook, stirring occasionally, until the apples are steamed and very soft, about 20 minutes. Uncover, increase the heat to medium-high, and cook, stirring often, until the apples are broken down and beginning to brown and stick to the bottom of the pan. Remove from the heat, discard the vanilla bean, and transfer to a food processor. Process until smooth, then transfer to a glass jar and seal with a lid. Store in the refrigerator for up to 2 weeks.

# HOMEMADE PANCAKE SYRUP

MAKES ABOUT 2½ CUPS

My go-to biscuit condiment has always been pancake syrup, but the stuff in bottles is hardly natural or remotely as tasty as my homemade kind made with browned butter, which adds depth and richness.

½ cup (1 stick) unsalted butter

2 cups packed light brown sugar

1 teaspoon kosher salt

Heat the butter in a small saucepan over medium-high heat and whisk often until the butter begins to brown and smell nutty. Immediately pour into a glass measuring cup and let cool for about 20 minutes to allow the solids to separate from the liquid. Using a spoon, scoop off and discard the white solids that float to the top. Pour the liquid butter back into a cleaned saucepan, adding or leaving behind the browned butter solids at the bottom (depending on how you want the syrup to look). Stir in the brown sugar, 1 cup water, and the salt. Heat over medium heat, stirring often, until the mixture begins to simmer and the sugar is dissolved. Pour into a clean heatproof glass jar and put a lid on the jar. Store at room temperature for up to 2 weeks or in the refrigerator for up to 2 months.

# STRAWBERRY-TOMATO-PEPPER JAM

MAKES ABOUT 4 CUPS

Even in the summertime when the weather is hot, I love biscuits! Fresh fruit preserves, such as this spicy-sweet jam, are perfect spread on hot or cold biscuits and make delicious use of the bounty from southern farmstands. If you want a sweeter, more pronounced berry flavor in this jam, omit the chiles and add 2 tablespoons framboise or Chambord liqueur while pureeing it in the food processor.

2 pounds ripe strawberries, fresh or frozen then thawed, hulled and halved

1 pound ripe summer tomatoes, cored and seeded

1 to 2 ripe red jalapeño or Fresno chiles, stemmed and finely chopped (use 1 chile for less heat, and omit the ribs and seeds altogether for a mild jam)

2 cups sugar

1 teaspoon kosher salt

1 cup fresh orange juice

¼ vanilla bean, seeds scraped and reserved

In a medium-size saucepan, combine all the ingredients and stir until evenly combined. Let sit to allow the sugar to pull some juices from the strawberries and tomatoes, about 10 minutes. Place the pan over medium-low heat and cover the pan. Cook, stirring occasionally, until the fruit is broken down and very soft, about 10 minutes. Uncover, increase the heat to medium-high, and cook, stirring often, until the fruit just begins to stick to the bottom of the pan. Remove from the heat, discard the vanilla bean, and transfer to a food processor. Process until smooth, then transfer to a clean heatproof glass jar and put a lid on the jar. Store in the refrigerator for up to 2 weeks.

# Corn Bread Pudding

WITH WHISKEY CARAMEL SAUCE

SERVES 8 TO 10

Every year at Thanksgiving, my family asks me to make a bread pudding using whatever leftover bread we have around after the big meal—sliced bread, biscuits, corn bread, even crackers have been pressed into service. Seeing how the same recipe varied year to year opened my eyes to the wide world of substitutions and variations, but my favorite version is this one, made entirely with homemade corn bread. The bread pudding will disappear fast enough on its own, but topped with Whiskey Caramel Sauce, it's a truly decadent dessert that belies its humble origins as a solution for leftovers.

---

Corn Bread (recipe follows), day-old, cut into 2- to 3-inch cubes

½ cup (1 stick) unsalted butter

2 cups milk

1 cup sugar

1 tablespoon vanilla extract

1½ teaspoons kosher salt

5 large eggs

Whiskey Caramel Sauce (recipe follows)

Heat the oven to 375°F.

Put the corn bread in a 3-quart oval or rectangular baking dish. Heat the butter in a small saucepan over medium-high heat, stirring often, until it begins to brown lightly. Remove from the heat and stir in the milk, sugar, vanilla, and salt, stirring until the sugar dissolves. Stir in the eggs, then pour over the corn bread. Let sit for about 10 minutes to allow the corn bread to soak up the custard, then cover with a sheet of aluminum foil. Bake for 30 minutes, remove the foil, then continue to bake until golden brown and set, about 30 minutes more. Let cool for about 10 minutes before serving, drizzled with the sauce.

# CORN BREAD

MAKES ONE 12-INCH ROUND LOAF OF CORN BREAD

1 cup yellow cornmeal,
   plus more for sprinkling

1 cup all-purpose flour

1 tablespoon baking powder

1 teaspoon kosher salt

¼ teaspoon baking soda

2 cups buttermilk

2 large eggs

½ cup (1 stick) unsalted butter

Heat the oven to 425°F.

In a large bowl, whisk together the cornmeal, flour, baking powder, salt, and baking soda. In another bowl, whisk together the buttermilk and eggs, then add to the dry ingredients and stir together until just combined.

Heat a 12-inch cast-iron skillet over medium-high heat until it just begins to smoke. Add the butter and swirl the pan constantly until the butter is completely melted. Pour the melted butter into the batter and stir to combine. Sprinkle the bottom of the skillet lightly with more cornmeal, then pour in the batter, smoothing the top quickly. Bake until a toothpick inserted in the middle comes out clean and the edges are golden brown, 25 to 30 minutes. Like biscuits, corn bread is best as soon as it comes out of the oven, so enjoy it right away with butter, or let it cool completely and sit out for a day to get stale to make Corn Bread Pudding.

# WHISKEY CARAMEL SAUCE

MAKES ABOUT 2 CUPS

1½ cups sugar

½ cup heavy cream

½ cup (1 stick) unsalted butter,
   cut into cubes

¼ cup whiskey, Bourbon, or Armagnac

¼ teaspoon kosher salt

¼ teaspoon freshly grated nutmeg

1 large egg, lightly beaten

In a small saucepan, stir together 1 cup of the sugar and ¼ cup water over medium-high heat until the sugar dissolves, then cook, without stirring, until the sugar turns a medium-amber color, about 10 minutes. Remove from the heat and add the cream, butter, whiskey, salt, and nutmeg and stir until smooth. In a medium-size heatproof bowl, whisk the remaining ½ cup sugar and the egg together until smooth, then drizzle in the warm caramel sauce and whisk well. Pour back into the saucepan and return to medium heat; cook, stirring often, until thickened, about 2 minutes. Serve the sauce immediately, spooned over bread pudding or ice cream, or pour into a clean heatproof glass jar and put a lid on the jar. Store in the refrigerator for up to 1 month.

# Pecan and Syrup Pancake Stack

MAKES ONE 9-INCH CAKE

Some say this decadent recipe—fresh pancakes stacked in a cake pan, layered with bananas and pecans, and soaked in homemade pancake syrup—is too over the top for breakfast and too breakfast-y for dessert. I say, "Who cares?" and make it anytime I want. You can refrigerate it overnight and simply reheat it in the oven in the morning to make a faux breakfast bread pudding or cake that is every bit the sweet indulgence I want from my pancakes.

4 cups all-purpose flour

1 tablespoon sugar

2 teaspoons kosher salt

2 cups plain natural yogurt

4 teaspoons baking soda

1 cup seltzer water or club soda

4 large eggs, lightly beaten

¾ cup (1½ sticks) unsalted butter

2½ cups Homemade Pancake Syrup (page 120), plus more for drizzling

1 cup roughly chopped toasted pecans

Banana slices

In a large bowl, combine the flour, sugar, and salt. In another bowl, stir together the yogurt and baking soda and let sit for 10 minutes. Stir in the seltzer and eggs, then pour it all over the dry ingredients and whisk until just combined. Let the batter rest for 10 minutes.

Spray a 9-inch round cake pan evenly with baking spray.

Heat 1 tablespoon of the butter in a 12-inch nonstick skillet over medium heat. Ladle about ½ cup of the batter into the skillet, gently spreading out the batter with the bottom of a spoon or a measuring cup to make an evenly flat disk. Cook the pancake until bubbles begin to form around the edge, about 2 minutes. Flip the pancake with a spatula and cook until golden brown, about 2 minutes more. Transfer the pancake to the prepared cake pan and drizzle with about 2 tablespoons of the syrup. Wipe out the skillet and repeat with the remaining butter and batter to make 12 pancakes total, layering each pancake on top of the other in the cake pan and drizzling syrup onto each.

If making ahead, once all the pancakes are made and in the pan with the syrup, cover the pan with plastic wrap and refrigerate overnight.

Heat the oven to 350°F. Unwrap the pan, pour ½ cup of the remaining syrup over the top of the pancake stack, and bake for 10 minutes. Pour the remaining ½ cup syrup over the stack and continue to bake until hot in the center, about 10 minutes more.

Let cool for 5 minutes. Place a warmed plate upside down over the pancake stack and, using pot holders or towels, carefully invert them together, then remove the pan. Cut the stack into 8 large wedges, drizzle with more syrup, then top with the pecans. Serve each wedge on a plate with bananas and, if you're like me, yet another drizzle of syrup.

# Cream Cheese-Layered Cinnamon Rolls

MAKES 8 LARGE CINNAMON ROLLS

When I first developed these rolls, I wanted to incorporate cream cheese into them, but not in the normal guise as icing. To make better use of its moistening stabilizers, I decided to laminate it, puff pastry dough–style, into a butter-rich bun dough. The result is a cinnamon roll that stays soft and tender long after it's baked. A tangy buttermilk glaze offsets the sugary filling, but make sure to make these for a crowd: You don't want to be tempted with the whole pan in front of you first thing in the morning.

FOR THE DOUGH:

1 (¼-ounce) package active
    dry yeast

¼ cup granulated sugar

½ cup milk, heated to 115°F

2 tablespoons light brown sugar

½ teaspoon vanilla extract

1 large whole egg

1 large egg yolk

2¾ cups all-purpose flour, plus
    more for the work surface

1 teaspoon kosher salt

½ cup (1 stick) unsalted butter,
    at room temperature

4 ounces cream cheese,
    at room temperature

MAKE THE DOUGH: In the bowl of a stand mixer fitted with the dough hook, combine the yeast, a pinch of the granulated sugar, and the milk. Stir to combine, then let sit until foamy, about 10 minutes. Add the remaining granulated sugar, the brown sugar, vanilla, whole egg, and egg yolk and stir until smooth. Add the flour and salt and mix on medium speed until the dough just comes together. Increase the speed to medium-high and knead the dough for 4 minutes. Add the butter and continue kneading until the dough is smooth and pulls away from the side of the bowl, about 6 minutes more. Remove the bowl from the mixer, cover with plastic wrap, and let sit in a warm place until doubled in size, 1½ to 2 hours.

MEANWHILE, START THE FILLING: In a bowl, combine the granulated sugar, brown sugar, pecans, cinnamon, salt, and cloves. Add the maple syrup and stir to combine.

Spray a 9-by-13-inch baking pan evenly with baking spray.

Punch down the dough and transfer it to a heavily floured surface. Gently knead the dough until it's no longer sticky, adding more flour as necessary, about 1 minute. Using a floured rolling pin, roll the dough into a 10-inch square. In a small bowl, beat the cream cheese with a wooden spoon or rubber spatula until it's spreadable. Spread the cream cheese evenly over the dough square, then fold

½ cup granulated sugar

¼ cup packed dark brown sugar

½ cup finely chopped pecans

1 tablespoon ground cinnamon

½ teaspoon kosher salt

⅛ teaspoon ground cloves

2 tablespoons maple syrup

½ cup (1 stick) unsalted butter, melted

FOR THE ICING:

2 cups confectioners' sugar

¼ cup buttermilk

the square into thirds as you would fold a letter. Take the open ends of the resulting rectangle and fold into thirds again, to make a small dough square. Invert the dough square so that the seam is down and let sit for about 10 minutes to relax the gluten. Using the rolling pin, gently roll the square into a 10-by-20-inch rectangle.

Turn the dough so that one of the short sides is closest to you. Brush the dough with half of the melted butter. Sprinkle the filling over the dough, leaving a 1-inch border at the edge farthest away from you, then lightly press the filling into the dough. Using your hands, lift up the bottom edge of the dough and roll it forward into a cylinder. Place the dough cylinder, seam side down, on a cutting board and, using a thin, sharp knife, trim off the ends; cut the cylinder crosswise into 8 equal-size slices. Nestle the slices, cut sides up and evenly spaced from one another, into the prepared baking pan. Cover with plastic wrap and let sit in a warm place to rise until doubled in size, about 2 hours. (An even better idea is to let the rolls rise overnight in the refrigerator, at least 8 hours or up to 12.)

Heat the oven to 375°F.

Uncover the rolls and, if you refrigerated them, let them sit at room temperature for 15 minutes to take the chill off. Bake until golden brown and a toothpick inserted in the middle of the rolls comes out clean, about 30 minutes.

MEANWHILE, MAKE THE ICING: In a small bowl, whisk together the confectioners' sugar and buttermilk until smooth.

Brush the hot rolls with the remaining ¼ cup butter, drizzle with the icing, and serve immediately.

# Edam Cheese Rolls

Growing up, we had big balls of red wax–covered Edam cheese around our house constantly, thanks to the college dairy that sold them at my parents' alma mater. But it wasn't until a few years ago, when working on a recipe for Filipino brioche rolls that use Edam, that I truly awakened to the cheese's unique character and the delicious quality it brings to breads and rolls. I serve these rolls, which are much more substantial than a gougère, as a passed appetizer at parties or as a breakfast roll, split and stuffed with sausage or bacon and a folded omelet.

½ cup milk

1 (¼-ounce) package active dry yeast

1 tablespoon sugar

6 large egg yolks, at room temperature

2 teaspoons dry mustard

4 tablespoons (½ stick) unsalted butter, melted, plus more for the pan

2 cups all-purpose flour

1 teaspoon kosher salt

8 ounces grated aged Edam cheese

Egg wash (see page 80)

In the bowl of a stand mixer fitted with the paddle attachment, combine the milk, yeast, and sugar; stir together and let sit until foamy, about 10 minutes. Stir in the egg yolks, mustard, and butter, then add the flour and salt and mix with the paddle until a dough forms. Replace the paddle with the dough hook attachment and knead on medium speed until the butter is incorporated and the dough is smooth and elastic, about 8 minutes. Add the cheese and mix until evenly combined. Remove the bowl from the mixer, cover with plastic wrap, and let the dough sit until doubled in size, about 1 hour.

Heat the oven to 350°F. Grease a 9-inch round cake or spring-form pan with butter.

Transfer the dough to a work surface and divide into 12 equal portions. Roll each portion into a ball and place in the prepared pan; cover loosely with plastic wrap and let sit until risen slightly, about 40 minutes. Uncover and brush the buns with egg wash, then bake, rotating the pan halfway through, until golden brown, about 40 minutes. Transfer to a wire rack and let cool completely.

# German Sugar Bread

MAKES ONE 9-BY-5-INCH LOAF

I can say with certainty that this bread changed my life. Since the first bite, eaten at a friend's restaurant in New York City a couple years ago, this soft, sweet, traditional German white bread enveloping cinnamon-laced sugar chunks has become the stuff of my dreams. When my friend Arlyn Blake, who wrote *The I Love to Cook Book* in 1971, gave me the recipe, I had to include it here. Just like Arlyn, this bread is smart, simple, stylish, and sweet. You'll dream about it too, once you try it.

1 (¼-ounce) package active dry yeast

⅛ teaspoon ground ginger

½ cup milk, heated to 115°F

½ cup warm water

2 tablespoons unsalted butter, softened

2 tablespoons sugar

2 teaspoons kosher salt

3 cups all-purpose flour

½ cup broken sugar cubes

2 teaspoons ground cinnamon

Egg wash (see page 80)

In the bowl of a stand mixer fitted with the paddle attachment, combine the yeast, ginger, and milk; stir together and let sit until foamy, about 10 minutes. Stir in the water, butter, sugar, and salt, then add the flour and mix with the paddle until a dough forms. Replace the paddle with the dough hook attachment and knead on medium speed until the butter is incorporated and the dough is smooth and elastic, about 8 minutes. Remove the bowl from the mixer, cover with plastic wrap, and let the dough sit until doubled in size, about 1 hour.

Heat the oven to 400°F. Spray a 9-by-5inch loaf pan evenly with baking spray.

Transfer the dough to a work surface and punch it down into a flat round. Toss the sugar cube pieces and the cinnamon together in a small bowl until evenly coated, then pour over the dough and fold and knead just enough to incorporate the sugar pieces evenly into the dough. Form into a thick log and place in the prepared loaf pan; cover loosely with plastic wrap and let sit until the dough has risen slightly, about 1 hour. Uncover and brush with egg wash, then bake for 10 minutes; lower the oven temperature to 350°F and continue to bake until the loaf has risen and is golden brown, about 35 minutes. Transfer to a wire rack and let cool completely before slicing into thick slabs for breakfast.

# Orange Breakfast Rolls

MAKES 16 ROLLS

We had Sister Schubert's orange rolls on the breakfast table every weekend and I never got tired of them. I couldn't get enough of the soft yeast rolls filled with orange butter in place of cinnamon, and this is my version of this nostalgic childhood treat. It still hits the spot whenever I get a craving for intense orange flavor first thing in the morning.

## FOR THE DOUGH:

⅔ cup milk

1 (¼-ounce) package active dry yeast

3 tablespoons sugar

1 tablespoon unsalted butter, melted

1½ teaspoons kosher salt

2 large egg whites, lightly beaten

2⅔ cups all-purpose flour

## FOR THE FILLING:

1 cup (2 sticks) unsalted butter, softened

¼ cup granulated sugar

Grated zest of 2 oranges

1½ cups confectioners' sugar

1 tablespoon fresh orange juice

½ teaspoon vanilla extract

MAKE THE DOUGH: In the bowl of a stand mixer fitted with the dough hook, stir together the milk, yeast, and a pinch of the sugar; let sit until foamy, about 10 minutes. Add the remaining sugar, the melted butter, salt, and egg whites and stir until smooth. Add the flour and mix on medium speed until the dough just comes together. Increase the speed to medium-high and knead until the dough is smooth and pulls away from the side of the bowl, about 8 minutes more. Remove the bowl from the mixer, cover with plastic wrap, and let sit in a warm place until doubled in size, 1½ to 2 hours.

MEANWHILE, MAKE THE FILLING: In a large bowl, beat the butter, granulated sugar, and orange zest with a handheld mixer on high speed until smooth. Add the confectioners' sugar, orange juice, and vanilla and beat until smooth. Place ⅓ cup in a separate bowl and cover with plastic wrap.

Transfer the dough to a work surface and punch it down into a flat circle. Cut the circle into 16 equal pieces, then shape each one into a rough rope and tie into a knot. Place the knots in the larger bowl of orange butter and toss gently with your hands until they're all coated in orange butter. Transfer them to an 8-inch square glass baking dish, spreading them out evenly, and cover with plastic wrap. Let sit until slightly risen, about 1 hour at room temperature or about 8 hours in the refrigerator (or overnight).

Heat the oven to 350°F. Uncover the rolls and, if you refrigerated them, let them sit at room temperature for about 15 minutes to take the chill off, then bake until golden brown and cooked through, 25 to 30 minutes. Remove from the oven and immediately dollop small spoonfuls of the reserved orange butter over the rolls, letting the butter melt on top of and between the rolls. Let cool for at least 15 minutes before serving the rolls warm.

# New Orleans King Cake

SERVES 12 TO 16

Many food snobs who know king cake, and even many who live in New Orleans, would laugh to hear someone actually profess to cherish it, but it's more than just nostalgia for me. I immediately hear a blast of trumpeted jazz music and see the green, purple, and gold colors of the season flash in front of my eyes. Like a giant sweet roll in ring form, sweetened brioche-style bread dough is filled with infinitely variable fillings, from simple and pristine cinnamon sugar to irresistibly indulgent cream cheese–praline, and formed into a large ring that's gilded with icing and green, purple, and yellow sugars.

FOR THE DOUGH:

1 (¼-ounce) package active dry yeast

6 tablespoons sugar

¾ cup milk

1 large egg

1 large egg yolk

2¾ cups all-purpose flour,
    plus more for the work surface

1 teaspoon kosher salt

½ cup (1 stick) unsalted butter, softened

FOR THE FILLING:

2 (8-ounce) packages cream cheese

½ cup packed dark brown sugar

½ cup chopped pecans

2 teaspoons ground cinnamon

1 teaspoon kosher salt

Grated zest of 1 lemon

FOR THE ICING:

2 cups confectioners' sugar

¼ cup buttermilk

Green, purple, and yellow sanding sugars

MAKE THE DOUGH: In the bowl of a stand mixer fitted with the dough hook attachment, combine the yeast, a pinch of the sugar, and the milk. Stir to combine and let sit until foamy, about 10 minutes. Add the remaining sugar, the egg, and egg yolk and stir until smooth. Add the flour and salt and mix on medium speed until the dough just comes together. Increase the speed to medium-high and knead the dough for 4 minutes. Add the butter and continue kneading until the dough is smooth and pulls away from the side of the bowl, about 6 minutes more. Remove the bowl from the mixer, cover with plastic wrap, and let sit in a warm place until doubled in size, 1½ to 2 hours.

MEANWHILE, MAKE THE FILLING: In a bowl, combine the cream cheese, brown sugar, pecans, cinnamon, salt, and lemon zest and beat with a handheld mixer until smooth.

Punch down the dough and place it on a heavily floured work surface. Gently knead the dough until it's no longer sticky, adding more flour as necessary, about 1 minute. Using a floured rolling pin, roll the dough into a 10-by-20-inch rectangle. Turn the dough so that one of the short sides is closest to you. Spread the filling over the dough, leaving a 1-inch border along both of the longer sides, but spreading the filling all the way to the edge on the shorter sides. Using your hands, lift up the bottom edge of the dough and roll it forward into a cylinder. Place the dough cylinder, seam side down, on a parchment paper–lined baking sheet and join the two ends, pressing them together and partly overlapping their edges, until you have an elongated oval. Cover with plastic wrap and let the dough sit in a warm place to rise until slightly risen, 1 to 1½ hours. (An even better idea is to let it rise overnight in the refrigerator, at least 8 hours or up to 12.)

Heat the oven to 350°F.

Uncover the king cake and, if you refrigerated it, let it sit at room temperature for 15 minutes to take the chill off. Bake until golden brown and a toothpick inserted in the middle comes out clean, about 30 minutes. Let cool to room temperature.

MAKE THE ICING: In a small bowl, whisk together the confectioners' sugar and buttermilk until smooth.

Drizzle the cake with the icing and sprinkle with the sanding sugars. Let sit to firm the icing before serving.

TIP: If you want to hide a small trinket inside the cake, which is very traditional (the finder becomes king for a day or, in my world, is responsible for bringing the next king cake to the next party), place a whole pecan half, a large dried kidney bean, or a small plastic baby (representing baby Jesus) in the filling once it's spread on the dough and roll up the dough as usual. Just remember to tell your guests it's in there so they can look for it and don't swallow their piece in one bite, like I would.

# Peach Melba Summer Pudding

SERVES 8 TO 10

A British classic of simple cooked fruit layered with bread and chilled until firm, summer pudding could quite possibly be the easiest and most gratifying dessert I've ever made and eaten. Here, I substitute raspberries for the traditional currants in the sauce and layer it with good-quality white bread and peaches for a spin on the classic peach Melba flavors. Feel free to use brioche or another soft country bread, but the allure of this dessert is its simplicity.

---

4 half-pints fresh raspberries

1 cup sugar

¼ cup peach schnapps

Juice of 1 lemon

½ teaspoon kosher salt

1 whole loaf white sandwich bread (1½ pounds)

4 pounds peeled and pitted peaches, roughly chopped

Sweetened whipped cream for serving

In a large saucepan, combine the raspberries, sugar, schnapps, lemon juice, and salt and cook over medium heat until the sugar is dissolved and the berries break down, about 10 minutes. Remove from the heat and let cool to room temperature.

Slice the bread into ½-inch-thick slices and remove the crusts (or keep them on, if you like). Line a large bowl, either a 7-inch-diameter soufflé dish or just a large prep bowl, preferably with a somewhat flat bottom and steeply sloping sides, with plastic wrap, leaving plenty of overhang on the sides. Arrange the bread slices neatly in the bottom and then ladle some of the raspberry sauce over the bread to saturate it. Distribute some peach pieces over the sauce, then continue layering bread, (cutting it to fit), berry sauce, and peaches until all the ingredients are used, making sure you end with sauce.

Fold the overhanging edges of plastic wrap over the top of the pudding and then cover with another sheet of plastic wrap. Over the pudding, place a flat plate that just fits over it and doesn't touch the bowl, and weigh it down with a cast-iron skillet or a couple of large cans. Refrigerate the pudding for at least 8 hours or up to overnight, then remove the weight and keep refrigerated until ready to serve.

When ready to serve, unwrap the pudding on top, place a large platter or serving plate upside down over the pudding, then invert the plate and bowl together, letting the pudding fall onto the plate. Remove the bowl and peel away the plastic wrap. Place large dollops of whipped cream over the top and spread evenly to cover the top. Serve in large wedges or use a large spoon to scoop out big mounds of pudding and serve in bowls with more whipped cream.

# Strawberry Grunt

SERVES 8

I'm a sucker for the combination of strawberries and cream. This boiled and baked fruit dessert combines that pair in stellar form: bubbling strawberry jam beneath sweet cream biscuits. Serve it up piping hot out of the oven and forget all your worries, if only for a while.

1 cup all-purpose flour

1¼ cups sugar, plus more
for sprinkling

2¼ teaspoons baking powder

1½ teaspoons kosher salt

2 tablespoons cold unsalted
butter, cut into cubes

²/₃ cup heavy cream

2 pounds strawberries,
hulled and quartered

1½ cups fresh orange juice

Vanilla Soft-Serve
(page 206; optional)

In a bowl, whisk together the flour, ¼ cup of the sugar, the baking powder, and ½ teaspoon of the salt; add the butter and, using your fingers, rub the butter into the flour until it forms pea-size crumbles. Add the cream and stir just until a moist dough forms. Refrigerate until ready to use or for up to 8 hours.

Heat the oven to 400°F.

In a 12-inch cast-iron or enamelware skillet, combine the remaining 1 cup sugar and 1 teaspoon salt, along with the strawberries and orange juice, and bring to a boil over high heat, stirring to dissolve the sugar. Cook for about 5 minutes, until the strawberries begin to break down slightly. Remove from the heat and, using a 1-ounce ice cream scoop or two tablespoons, portion and form the chilled dough into 2-inch dumplings and drop them on top of the strawberries, spacing them evenly apart. Sprinkle the dumplings with more sugar, then transfer the skillet to the oven. Bake until the biscuits are golden brown and cooked through and the strawberries are reduced and bubbly, about 25 minutes.

Let cool for about 10 minutes, then serve hot with a large scoop of soft-serve, if you like.

# Custards & Puddings

AMBROSIA PAVLOVA

BUTTERMILK ÎLE FLOTTANTE

PURE AND SINFUL TRIFLE

MINT JULEP CRÈME BRÛLÉE

REVERSED IMPOSSIBLE CHOCOLATE FLAN

SATSUMA WHIPPED RICE PUDDING

SWEET POTATO PUDDINGS

WATERMELON GELATIN

# Ambrosia Pavlova

SERVES 8

Church potlucks in the South are never complete without ambrosia salad, a concoction of sweetened shredded coconut, canned pineapple and orange segments, marshmallows, pistachios or pecans, and sometimes red maraschino cherries. Always the joke of the buffet, it still somehow seemed to get polished off by the end of the meal. I've always been drawn to its potential as a dessert, specifically as pavlova, the New Zealand dessert of crunchy meringue topped with cream and fresh fruit.

You can make the meringue disk and pineapple curd up to 2 days in advance (wrap the meringue loosely in plastic wrap and store in a dry place). However, once assembled, serve the pavlova immediately to ensure that the meringue stays crisp and crunchy against the soft whipped cream and juicy fruit. If your meringue disk breaks into a million pieces or cracks horribly beyond repair, don't worry. There's a lovely dessert the British call Eton mess, basically all the components of pavlova stirred together and served in a glass like a pudding. So, break your meringue into even more bite-size pieces and layer them parfait style in milk shake glasses with the whipped cream, curd, fruit, and coconut, and dig in with a long-handled spoon.

FOR THE PINEAPPLE CURD:

¼ cup sugar

¼ teaspoon kosher salt

Grated zest of 1 lemon

1 large egg yolk

¼ cup fresh pineapple juice

2 tablespoons unsalted butter, melted

FOR THE MERINGUE:

¼ cup cornstarch

1 tablespoon distilled white vinegar

1 tablespoon vanilla extract

1 teaspoon kosher salt

2 cups sugar

8 large egg whites, at room temperature

1 cup very finely ground pistachios, toasted and cooled

MAKE THE PINEAPPLE CURD: In a small saucepan, whisk together the sugar, salt, lemon zest, and egg yolk until smooth. Add the pineapple juice and butter and stir until smooth. Bring to a simmer over medium heat, stirring constantly. Once it begins to simmer, continue to cook and stir the curd until it is thickened and coats the back of a spoon, about 2 minutes. Transfer to a bowl and let cool to room temperature. Cover with plastic wrap and refrigerate until ready to use.

MAKE THE MERINGUE: Heat the oven to 350°F.

In a small bowl, stir together the cornstarch, vinegar, vanilla, and salt until a thick paste forms. Put the sugar and egg whites in the bowl of a stand mixer fitted with the whisk attachment and mix on low speed until smooth. Increase the speed to medium-high and beat until soft peaks form. Add the cornstarch paste to the beating egg whites and continue to beat until very stiff and glossy peaks form, about 5 minutes. Add the pistachios and, using a rubber spatula, very gently fold until evenly incorporated.

FOR THE TOPPING:

¼ cup sugar

Grated zest of 2 oranges

½ teaspoon kosher salt

½ cup unsweetened coconut milk

1 cup cold heavy cream

1 orange, peeled of its pith and cut into segments

1 grapefruit, peeled of its pith and cut into segments

½ cup candied cherries in syrup, such as Amarena Fabbri, or fresh or thawed frozen pitted cherries

Large dried coconut shavings

Julienned lime zest

Chopped pistachios

Trace a 9-inch circle onto a sheet of parchment paper. Flip the sheet over and transfer it to a baking sheet; spray lightly with baking spray. Pile the meringue in the center of the circle and, using an offset spatula or small rubber spatula, form it into a 9-inch disk, smoothing the top and sides. Transfer to the oven and immediately lower the oven temperature to 215°F. Bake until the meringue is dried on the outside and looks set, about 1½ hours. Without opening the door, turn the oven off and let the meringue sit inside until completely cooled, at least 4 hours. (The cooling process allows the meringue to dry and cool slowly enough so that it doesn't collapse on itself.) Once cooled, gently tip the meringue onto its side and peel away the parchment paper. Carefully place the meringue on a flat cake stand or serving platter.

WHEN READY TO SERVE, MAKE THE WHIPPED CREAM: In a food processor, combine the sugar, orange zest, salt, and coconut milk in a food processor and process until the sugar is dissolved and the zest heavily perfumes the coconut milk. Pour into a large bowl, add the cream, and whisk until stiff peaks form. Pile the whipped cream onto the center of the meringue and gently nudge it to the edge of the meringue, leaving about a 1½-inch border.

Arrange the orange and grapefruit segments on the cream and then drizzle with some of the pineapple curd. Dot the top with cherries, coconut, lime zest, and more chopped pistachios and serve immediately.

# Buttermilk Île Flottante

(BUTTERMILK CUSTARD WITH NUTMEG MERINGUES)

SERVES 8

I'm one of those weird people who just love meringue. Don't ask me why, but I could literally eat bowls of the stuff. It is, after all, just sugar and air trapped in egg whites. It doesn't require a lot of thought or concentration to enjoy, and sometimes that's what you want in a dessert. Here, a pool of pleasantly tangy vanilla custard encircles a nutmeg-suffused meringue island, torched to caramel-y, burnt-marshmallow perfection.

Although not shown in the photograph, the caramelized pecans here make an ideal crunchy garnish.

FOR THE CUSTARD:

4 large egg yolks

1 cup sugar

1 vanilla bean, split, seeds scraped and reserved

2 cups buttermilk

1 cup heavy cream

½ cup sour cream

1 tablespoon vanilla extract

FOR THE MERINGUE:

1 cup sugar

4 large egg whites

½ teaspoon cream of tartar

1 teaspoon freshly grated nutmeg

¼ teaspoon ground allspice

FOR GARNISH:

Sugared Pecans, optional (recipe follows)

MAKE THE CUSTARD: In a medium-size saucepan, whisk together the egg yolks, sugar, and vanilla bean with seeds until smooth and light, at least 1 minute. Add the buttermilk and whisk until smooth. Place over medium heat and cook, stirring often with a rubber spatula, until the mixture thickens slightly and coats the back of a spoon (you'll also know the custard is almost ready when the foam on the surface disappears and the mixture stops moving abruptly after giving it a quick stir). Remove from the heat and pour through a fine-mesh sieve into a bowl. Add the cream, sour cream, and vanilla and stir until smooth. Refrigerate the custard until chilled, at least 2 hours.

MEANWHILE, MAKE THE MERINGUE: Put the sugar and ½ cup water in a small saucepan and bring to a boil, stirring to dissolve the sugar. Attach a candy thermometer to the side of the pan and cook, without stirring, until the syrup reaches 250°F. Before the syrup reaches the correct temperature, put the egg whites, cream of tartar, nutmeg, and allspice in the bowl of a stand mixer fitted with the whisk attachment and beat until soft peaks form. Once the syrup reaches 250°F, slowly drizzle it into the beating egg whites; continue beating until the mixture has cooled and is light and fluffy, about 5 minutes.

To serve, use a large serving spoon to drop large, oval-shaped dollops of the meringue into the center of individual serving plates (make sure the plates have at least a ¼-inch rim). Using a hand-held blowtorch, evenly brown the outsides of the meringues on each plate (see page 44). Pour the chilled custard around each meringue so it pools completely around the meringue "islands." Drape the pecans over the meringues and serve immediately.

NOTE: If you have any leftover custard, freeze it in an ice cream churn to make ice cream. Leftover meringue can be dolloped over fresh fruit, brownies, or pudding and browned for a decadent instant topping.

## SUGARED PECANS

½ cup sugar

½ cup whole pecan halves, toasted and cooled

Put the sugar in a small skillet and heat over medium-high heat, swirling the pan often, until the sugar melts into a liquid caramel. As soon as all the sugar is liquid, remove the skillet from the heat, stir in the pecans with a fork, then quickly drag the pecans from the skillet to a piece of parchment paper. You should get long strands of caramel that trail between the pecans and the skillet; these are good! Try to keep them intact: Once they're cool, you can decorate the meringues with the pecans, letting the caramel trail spikes shoot upward.

# Pure and Sinful Trifle

(DEVIL'S FOOD CAKE, ANGEL FOOD CAKE, PEANUT BUTTER MOUSSE, AND RASPBERRIES)

SERVES 10 TO 12

In this spin on Dallas-based chef Stephen Pyles's famous Heaven and Hell Cake, I layer angel food and devil's food with smooth peanut butter mousse in a towering trifle dish, and top it all with milk chocolate ganache. It's over-the-top indulgence of the best sort.

FOR THE ANGEL FOOD CAKE:

1½ cups confectioners' sugar

1 cup cake flour

1½ cups egg whites
(about 10-12 eggs)

1 teaspoon cream of tartar

⅛ teaspoon kosher salt

1 cup granulated sugar

2 teaspoons vanilla extract

1 teaspoon almond extract

FOR THE DEVIL'S FOOD CAKE:

1½ cups cake flour

1 teaspoon baking soda

¾ teaspoon kosher salt

¼ teaspoon baking powder

1 cup brewed coffee, cooled

½ cup Dutch-process cocoa powder, sifted

½ cup (1 stick) unsalted butter

1½ cups sugar

1 teaspoon vanilla extract

2 large eggs

MAKE THE ANGEL FOOD CAKE: Heat the oven to 325°F. Line the bottom of a 9-by-13-inch baking pan with parchment paper; do not grease or spray with baking spray.

In a bowl, sift together the confectioners' sugar and cake flour. In the bowl of a stand mixer fitted with the whisk attachment, beat the egg whites, cream of tartar, and salt on medium-high speed until soft peaks form. Sprinkle in the granulated sugar, vanilla, and almond extract and beat until stiff peaks form. Sprinkle half of the confectioners' sugar–flour mixture over the egg whites and use a rubber spatula to fold until just combined. Repeat with the remaining flour mixture, then pour the batter into the prepared pan and bake until the top of the cake is lightly browned and a toothpick inserted in the middle comes out clean, about 50 minutes. Let cool completely in the pan, then unmold the cake, trim off the edges, and cut into 1½-inch cubes.

MAKE THE DEVIL'S FOOD CAKE: Increase the oven temperature to 350°F. Spray a 9-by-13-inch baking pan with baking spray.

In a bowl, whisk together the cake flour, baking soda, salt, and baking powder. In another bowl, whisk together the coffee and cocoa powder until smooth. In the bowl of a stand mixer fitted with the paddle attachment, beat the butter, sugar, vanilla, and eggs on medium-high speed until pale and fluffy, about 4 minutes. Alternately add the dry ingredients and the coffee mixture and beat until evenly combined and smooth. Pour the batter into the prepared pan and bake until a toothpick inserted in the middle of the cake comes out clean, about 45 minutes. Let cool completely in the pan, then unmold the cake, trim off the edges, and cut into 1½-inch cubes.

**FOR THE PEANUT BUTTER MOUSE:**

2 (8-ounce) packages cream cheese,
  at room temperature

2⅔ cups smooth peanut butter,
  at room temperature

2½ cups confectioners' sugar, sifted

**FOR THE GANACHE:**

12 ounces milk chocolate,
  such as Valrhona, chopped

1½ cups heavy cream

**FOR SERVING:**

Whipped cream

Raspberries (optional)

MAKE THE PEANUT BUTTER MOUSSE: In the bowl of a stand mixer fitted with the paddle attachment, combine the cream cheese, peanut butter, and confectioners' sugar and beat on medium-high speed until smooth and fluffy, about 4 minutes.

MAKE THE GANACHE: Put the chocolate in a heatproof bowl. Bring the cream to a boil in a small saucepan, then pour it over the chocolate. Let sit for about 2 minutes to let the cream melt the chocolate, then, starting in the center, begin slowly whisking until the chocolate and cream emulsify and are smooth. Let cool for about 1 hour, stirring occasionally.

Place half of the devil's food cake cubes in the bottom of a 6-quart glass trifle dish and spread with one third of the peanut butter mousse. Top with half of the angel food cake cubes, then spread with half of the remaining mousse. Repeat with the remaining cake cubes and peanut butter mousse, ending with angel food cake. Pour the ganache evenly over the angel food cake, covering it evenly and allowing it to drizzle and pool down the insides of the trifle. Cover the top of the trifle with large dollops of whipped cream and sprinkle with raspberries to your liking, or leave them off altogether. Serve right away or refrigerate for up to 8 hours.

# Mint Julep Crème Brûlée

SERVES 6

There's nothing like a cooling mint julep on a hot, muggy southern night. I always thought crème brûlée was the perfect vehicle for those refreshing flavors in dessert form because burnt sugar mimics the caramelized flavors in Bourbon. At the end of a summer meal, this light, mint-perfumed custard is just as bewitching, but less inebriating, as the iconic cocktail.

4 cups heavy cream

1 vanilla bean, split,
    seeds scraped and reserved

1 bunch fresh mint,
    stems removed

¾ cup granulated sugar

2 tablespoons Bourbon

8 large egg yolks

Turbinado sugar

Heat the oven to 300°F.

Bring the cream and vanilla bean with seeds to a simmer in a medium-size saucepan, then remove from the heat, add the mint, and let sit for 1 hour.

In a bowl, combine the granulated sugar, Bourbon, and egg yolks and whisk until smooth. Pour the mint-flavored cream through a fine-mesh sieve into the bowl, pressing against the mint to extract as much liquid as possible; discard the mint.

Place a paper towel in the bottom of a 9-by-13-inch baking pan and place six 6-ounce ramekins inside the pan. Divide the custard evenly among the ramekins. Pour boiling water into the pan until it comes halfway up the sides of the ramekins. Bake until the custards are set but still slightly loose in the centers, about 35 minutes. Remove the ramekins from the pan and place them on a rimmed baking sheet. Immediately refrigerate and chill until firm, at least 4 hours.

Sprinkle turbinado sugar evenly over the surface of each custard and, using a handheld torch (see page 44), caramelize the sugar until it's browned and liquid. Let sit until the sugar hardens again, then serve immediately.

# Reversed Impossible Chocolate Flan

MAKES ONE 10-INCH BUNDT CAKE

Ever since I first ate "chocoflan," I was even more enamored with its flavor than the magic it undergoes while baking. Chocolate cake batter is placed in a pan and then vanilla custard is poured over the top; once the heat of the oven hits the batters, the heavier custard falls while the lighter batter rises, each solidifying into its respective layer. Reverse these flavors for my favorite iteration and add coconut. It doesn't get more magical than this.

FOR THE COCONUT CAKE BATTER:

1½ cups all-purpose flour

½ teaspoon baking powder

½ teaspoon baking soda

½ teaspoon kosher salt

¾ cup unsweetened coconut milk

1 tablespoon distilled white vinegar
    (or coconut vinegar, if you can get it)

1 teaspoon coconut extract

1 teaspoon vanilla extract

½ cup (1 stick) unsalted butter,
    at room temperature

¾ cup sugar

1 large egg

FOR THE CHOCOLATE CUSTARD:

1 (14-ounce) can sweetened
    condensed milk

1 (12-ounce) can evaporated milk

½ cup Dutch-process cocoa powder

1 teaspoon vanilla extract

4 large eggs

FOR SERVING:

Whiskey Caramel Sauce (page 124)

¼ cup chopped toasted pecans

MAKE THE COCONUT CAKE BATTER: Heat the oven to 375°F. Spray a 10-inch Bundt pan evenly with baking spray.

In a bowl, whisk together the flour, baking powder, baking soda, and salt. In another bowl, whisk together the coconut milk, vinegar, coconut extract, and vanilla. In a large bowl, combine the butter and sugar and beat with a handheld mixer on medium-high speed until pale and fluffy, about 4 minutes. Add the egg and beat until smooth. Add the dry ingredients and wet ingredients and beat until just combined. Pour the cake batter into the prepared pan and evenly distribute, smoothing the top. Set aside.

MAKE THE CHOCOLATE CUSTARD: Combine the condensed milk, evaporated milk, cocoa powder, vanilla, and eggs in a blender and blend until smooth. Hold a spoon upside down over the cake batter in the pan and gently pour the custard over the back of the spoon so that it lands gently on top of the cake batter without disturbing it. Set the pan in a large, high-sided roasting pan and transfer the pans to the middle rack of the oven. Pour enough boiling water into the large pan to come 1 inch up the side of the Bundt pan, then bake until a toothpick inserted in the cake comes out clean, about 45 minutes. Remove the Bundt pan from the water bath and transfer to a wire rack to cool completely.

Place a serving plate or platter upside down over the Bundt pan and carefully invert them together, letting the cake and flan fall to the platter. Gently remove the pan and then drizzle with the whiskey sauce and sprinkle with the pecans. Cut into large wedges to serve.

# Satsuma Whipped Rice Pudding

SERVES 12

Until experimenting with a Swedish technique while at *Saveur*, I'd thought rice pudding always meant the same hot, loose porridge with cinnamon and raisins. Instead, here cooled basmati rice is folded with whipped cream into a light, fluffy cloud topped with bright citrus segments and sweet jam. Louisiana-grown satsumas are an ideal complement to this rich pudding, their slightly bitter flesh and juice balanced perfectly by the preserves. If you can get your hands on some, try cloudberry preserves from Sweden.

---

1 cup basmati rice

1 teaspoon kosher salt

3 cups cold heavy cream

1 cup milk

2 cinnamon sticks

½ vanilla bean, split, seeds scraped and reserved

¾ cup sugar

2 satsumas or navel oranges, peeled and cut into segments

Fruit preserves, preferably cloudberry or raspberry (optional)

In a medium-size saucepan, combine the rice, salt, and 2 cups water and bring to a boil, stirring occasionally. Reduce the heat to low and simmer, stirring occasionally, until the water is absorbed, about 10 minutes. Stir in 2 cups of the cream, the milk, and cinnamon sticks and return to a boil. Reduce the heat to low, cover partially, and simmer, stirring occasionally, until the rice is cooked through and thickened, 30 to 35 minutes. Transfer the rice to a large bowl. Spread the rice out evenly and let cool, stirring occasionally, to room temperature.

In a medium-size bowl, whisk the remaining 1 cup cream and the vanilla seeds until soft peaks form. Slowly sprinkle the sugar into the cream while whisking and continue beating until stiff peaks form. Fold the whipped cream into the cooled rice, then ladle about ½ cup rice pudding into individual serving bowls. Divide the satsuma segments among the bowls and top with a dollop of preserves, if you like.

# Sweet Potato Puddings

WITH CASHEW CRUMBLE COOKIES

SERVES 8

Custard, in all its guises, is my favorite dessert. I'm constantly looking to transform every rich dessert into a pudding because sometimes you want a smooth, refreshing dessert over something hot out of the oven. So for Thanksgiving one year, I made this maple syrup–sweetened custard, an homage to sweet potato pie with caramelized roasted sweet potatoes (a great way to use up leftovers). The cookies can be crumbled into a topping to scatter over the pudding, or you can simply serve them on the side.

---

FOR THE CUSTARDS:

1 cup heavy cream

¾ cup milk

¾ cup maple syrup

½ cup pureed roasted sweet potatoes

8 large egg yolks

½ teaspoon kosher salt

½ teaspoon ground cinnamon

¼ teaspoon freshly grated nutmeg

FOR THE CRUMBLE COOKIES:

4 tablespoons (½ stick) unsalted butter, at room temperature

½ cup packed light brown sugar

¼ cup all-purpose flour

¾ cup roasted salted cashews, finely chopped

½ teaspoon vanilla extract

½ teaspoon kosher salt

MAKE THE CUSTARDS: Heat the oven to 325°F. Place about eight 6- to 8-ounce ramekins or custard cups in a large roasting pan.

In a bowl, combine the cream, milk, maple syrup, sweet potatoes, egg yolks, salt, cinnamon, and nutmeg and whisk until smooth. Divide among the ramekins, then place the roasting pan on the middle rack of the oven. Pour boiling water into the roasting pan, avoiding the ramekins, until it comes halfway up the sides of the ramekins. Close the oven door and bake until the custards are set but still jiggle slightly in the center when you tap their sides, about 35 minutes. Carefully remove the roasting pan from the oven and, using a kitchen towel or tongs, carefully lift each ramekin out of the water bath and onto a baking sheet. Transfer to the refrigerator and chill the custards until set and firm, at least 2 hours.

MAKE THE CRUMBLE COOKIES: Heat the oven to 350°F. Line a baking sheet with parchment paper.

In a bowl, combine the butter, brown sugar, flour, cashews, vanilla, and salt and rub and knead with your fingers until all the ingredients are evenly incorporated. Shape into 1-inch balls and place on the prepared baking sheet, spaced about 3 inches apart. Bake until spread out, golden brown, and crisp, about 12 minutes. Let cool completely, then serve crumbled over the custards or on the side.

# Watermelon Gelatin

When you have great sweet watermelon, you don't want to do too much to it. But sometimes you want more than just a raw slice. This simple, elegant preparation highlights the melon's fragrance and flavor, and the sea salt adds the perfect salty, crunchy counterpoint. Sweetened with a little sugar and vanilla, this gelatin dessert makes an elegant finish to a light summertime meal. With so few ingredients, the quality and ripeness of the watermelon and its juice are paramount to this dessert's success. To make the watermelon juice, coarsely chop the flesh, removing any large seeds, and puree in a blender until smooth; pour through a fine-mesh sieve to strain out the solids.

---

3 cups strained watermelon juice

1 tablespoon powdered gelatin

¾ cup sugar

1 teaspoon vanilla extract

Coarse sea salt

Put 2 cups of the watermelon juice in a bowl and sprinkle with the gelatin. Let sit for 5 minutes to allow the gelatin to soften. Put the remaining 1 cup juice and the sugar in a small saucepan and bring to a boil, stirring to dissolve the sugar. Remove from the heat and pour the mixture over the juice and gelatin in the bowl; add the vanilla and stir until the gelatin dissolves. Refrigerate the bowl of juice for 1 hour. Because the solids in the juice will settle as the juice sits, stir the juice again to make sure it's not separated, then divide the juice among whatever glasses you have—martini glasses, old-fashioned glasses, or custard cups—then refrigerate again until completely set, at least 4 hours.

To serve, simply sprinkle the tops of each glass with a tiny pinch of sea salt, or even more fresh-cut watermelon, if you like.

# Cookies & Confections

BIRTHDAY CAKE COOKIES

BRAZIL NUT–BUTTERSCOTCH BLONDIES

CHESTNUT BROWNIES

CHESS SQUARES

CHEWY WHITE CHOCOLATE GINGER COOKIES

HUSBAND'S DELIGHT

TEA CAKES

COCOONS

CREAM CHEESE SNICKERDOODLES

CRISP OATMEAL RAISIN COOKIES

GRAPEFRUIT-BLACKBERRY BARS

STRAWBERRY BARS

VEGAN BROWNIES

BUCKEYES

BUTTERMILK CARAMELS

MARBLED CHOCOLATE BARK

CHOCOLATE-COVERED MINTS

PRETZEL-PEANUT-CHOCOLATE CANDY

# Birthday Cake Cookies

MAKES ABOUT 36 COOKIES

Believe it or not, there are people in this world who don't want cake, even at a birthday party or wedding. To them I just shake my head and offer a plate of these elegant little cookies. They're just the thing for a low-key, grown-up party where you might be juggling finger food and a drink while talking with friends. They're small, not too sweet (perfect to nibble while imbibing), and are both festive and easy, like the best parties. To make them for a wedding or baby shower, use all white or pink and blue sprinkles.

4 cups all-purpose flour

1 tablespoon baking powder

1 teaspoon kosher salt

1½ cups (3 sticks) unsalted butter, softened

2 cups sugar

2 large eggs

2 tablespoons vanilla extract

Multicolored sprinkles

2 large egg whites, lightly beaten

Line baking sheets with parchment paper.

In a bowl, whisk together the flour, baking powder, and salt. Put the butter and sugar in a large bowl and beat with a handheld mixer on medium-high speed until pale and fluffy, about 2 minutes. Add the eggs and beat until smooth. Add the vanilla and then the dry ingredients and beat until just combined. Using a 2-ounce ice scream scoop or ¼-cup measuring cup, portion out the dough and shape each portion into a ball. Place the balls 2 inches apart on the prepared baking sheets. Lightly flour the bottom of a ¼-cup measuring cup and use it to press each ball into a flat disk; chill the disks for about 30 minutes.

Heat the oven to 375°F.

Put the sprinkles in a bowl. Using a pastry brush, lightly brush the top of a cookie disk with egg white. Press the top into the sprinkles so they completely cover the cookie. Return the cookie to the baking sheet, sprinkles side up, and repeat with the remaining cookies. Bake, rotating the baking sheets top to bottom and front to back halfway through, until set and lightly browned on the bottom, about 10 minutes. Let cool before serving.

# Brazil Nut–Butterscotch Blondies

SERVES 12 TO 16

Since I'm not a chocoholic myself, I've always enjoyed the pure, dense, molasses-y bite of a blondie to that of a brownie. Unfortunately, every recipe calls for packaged butterscotch chips, which taste horrendous, in my opinion. (They all contain food dyes that burn your throat after you swallow.) Fortunately, butterscotch chips aren't needed here, since butterscotch is basically the combination of butter and brown sugar. Good-quality white chocolate is never a bad addition in my book, and hearty Brazil nuts pack a warm depth here to offset all the sugar, but macadamia nuts, peanuts, cashews—any really buttery nut—can be used instead. Just don't use one with a tannic skin, like pecans or walnuts, which can intrude on the clean sugar flavor.

1 cup (2 sticks) unsalted butter

1¼ cups packed light brown sugar

½ cup granulated sugar

1 teaspoon vanilla extract

½ teaspoon kosher salt

4 large eggs

1 cup all-purpose flour

2 cups good-quality white chocolate chips

2 cups roughly chopped Brazil nuts

Heat the oven to 350°F. Spray a 9-by-13-inch baking pan evenly with baking spray.

Put the butter in a small saucepan and melt over medium heat, stirring often; cook until it begins to brown and smell nutty. Pour into a bowl. Add the brown sugar, granulated sugar, vanilla, and salt and stir until evenly combined. Add the eggs and whisk briskly until smooth and light, about twenty quick turns around the bowl. Add the flour, white chocolate chips, and Brazil nuts and stir until no pockets of flour remain. Pour the batter into the prepared pan and smooth the top. Bake until golden brown on top and a toothpick inserted in the middle comes out with just a few crumbs and a thin film of undercooked batter clinging to it, 35 to 40 minutes. Let cool completely before cutting into squares.

# Chestnut Brownies

SERVES 12 TO 16

I developed this recipe after baking a cake with chestnut flour and noticing that, when used alone, it lent the cake a dense, brownie-like fudginess and warm nutty flavor that I thought would work exceptionally well in a true brownie. And it's gluten-free, so anyone intolerant of wheat flour can enjoy these rich brownies, which in my opinion are even better than the traditional version.

---

4 cups chestnut flour

1 cup minced vacuum-packed chestnuts

½ cup Dutch-process cocoa powder

1 teaspoon kosher salt

2 cups sugar

1½ cups (3 sticks) unsalted butter, melted

1 cup milk

2 teaspoons vanilla extract

Heat the oven to 350°F. Spray a 9-by-13-inch baking pan evenly with baking spray.

In a bowl, whisk together the chestnut flour, chestnuts, cocoa powder, and salt. In another bowl, whisk together the sugar, butter, milk, and vanilla. Pour the wet ingredients over the dry ingredients and stir until smooth. Pour into the prepared baking pan and bake until a toothpick inserted in the middle comes out with just a few crumbs attached, about 30 minutes. Let cool completely before cutting into squares.

# Chess Squares

SERVES 16

I hate using the word "addictive" to describe food, but my god, if that isn't the first word that pops into my mind when I think of these insanely rich and gasp-inducing bars of heavenly manna. They're a favorite tailgate treat in the South, where they're made with boxed yellow cake mix. Through the magic of baking, they transform into a bar cookie version of chess pie that is, for lack of a better description, the love child of a stick of butter and cream cheese—in cake form.

2 cups all-purpose flour

1 tablespoon baking powder

½ teaspoon kosher salt

1½ cups granulated sugar

½ cup (1 stick) unsalted butter, at room temperature

2 teaspoons vanilla extract

4 large eggs

¼ cup milk

1 (8-ounce) package cream cheese, at room temperature

1 (1-pound) box confectioners' sugar, sifted

Heat the oven to 350°F. Line a 9-by-13-inch baking dish with parchment paper and spray evenly with baking spray.

In a bowl, whisk together the flour, baking powder, and salt. Put the granulated sugar, butter, and vanilla in the bowl of a stand mixer fitted with the paddle attachment and beat on medium-high speed until pale and fluffy. Add 1 of the eggs and beat until smooth. Add the dry ingredients and milk and beat on low speed until the dough just comes together and is smooth. Transfer the dough to the prepared baking dish and use your fingers to press it evenly into the bottom.

In a bowl, beat the cream cheese with a handheld mixer on medium-high speed until smooth and fluffy; add the remaining 3 eggs one at a time, beating well after each, until the mixture is smooth. Add the confectioners' sugar and beat on low speed until smooth (if a few lumps remain here and there, it's okay; they won't matter in the finished product). Pour the mixture over the dough in the baking dish and spread out evenly with a rubber spatula. Bake until a toothpick inserted in the middle comes out clean and the top is lightly browned, about 40 minutes. Let cool completely, then cut into about 16 small squares (you want to keep these rich bites small—trust me).

# Chewy White Chocolate Ginger Cookies

MAKES ABOUT 48 COOKIES

I love the combination of flavors in these rich cookies. The peppery sting of ginger is softened by the white chocolate's creamy sweetness. They're an obvious holiday cookie contender, but I may enjoy them even more with a glass of cold milk on a summer afternoon.

---

1¼ cups (2½ sticks) unsalted butter, softened

2 cups packed dark brown sugar

1 large egg

1 tablespoon grated peeled fresh ginger

1½ teaspoons grated lemon zest

4 cups all-purpose flour

2 teaspoons ground ginger

1 teaspoon ground cinnamon

1¼ teaspoons baking powder

¼ teaspoon ground cloves

½ teaspoon kosher salt

8 ounces good-quality white chocolate, finely chopped

Heat the oven to 350°F. Line baking sheets with parchment paper.

Put the butter and brown sugar in a bowl and beat with a handheld mixer on medium-high speed until pale and fluffy, about 2 minutes. Add the egg, fresh ginger, and lemon zest and beat until smooth. Add the flour, ground ginger, cinnamon, baking powder, cloves, and salt and beat until just combined. Stir in the chocolate until evenly incorporated. Using a 2-ounce ice cream scoop or ¼-cup measuring cup, portion out the dough and shape each portion into a ball. Place the balls 2 inches apart on the prepared baking sheets and bake, rotating the baking sheets halfway through, until set and lightly browned on the bottom, about 10 minutes. Remove to wire racks to cool.

PICTURED, FROM TOP LEFT:
Chewy White Chocolate Ginger Cookies, Cream Cheese Snickerdoodles (page 172), Crisp Oatmenal Raisin Cookies (pages 175), and Tea Cakes (page 169)

# Husband's Delight

MAKES 24 SQUARES

These cookies are basically an excuse to fill your house with that warming butter-cinnamon aroma. For all intents and purposes, they're just cinnamon pecan shortbread cookies. But my mom, long ago, accidentally baked a batch at about a hundred degrees less than she was supposed to, so when they were done, they were cooked but incredibly doughy and soft. They were so good that she kept making them this way. Somehow, some way, they attained the nickname "husband's delight" cookies, and that's what we always called them.

2 cups all-purpose flour

1 tablespoon plus 1 teaspoon ground cinnamon

1 teaspoon kosher salt

1 cup (2 sticks) unsalted butter

1 cup sugar

1 large egg, separated

2 cups whole pecans, roughly chopped

Heat the oven to 250°F. Line a 9-by-13-inch baking pan with parchment paper and spray evenly with baking spray.

In a bowl, whisk together the flour, cinnamon, and salt. In another bowl, combine the butter and sugar and beat with a handheld mixer on medium-high speed until smooth, pale, and fluffy, about 3 minutes. Add the egg yolk and beat until smooth. Add the dry ingredients and mix until just combined. Transfer to the prepared baking pan and press evenly into the bottom. Whisk the egg white until frothy, then pour it onto the dough and spread evenly with a pastry brush. Sprinkle the pecans evenly over the dough and press on them lightly with your hands so they adhere. Bake until set but still undercooked and soft, about 25 minutes. Let cool completely before cutting into squares.

# Tea Cakes

MAKES ABOUT 24 COOKIES

The first thing I ever learned to bake, these cookies are not only simple, they're simply heavenly. Because they're made with oil instead of butter, they're incredibly moist and taste purely of vanilla, almond, and sugar. I would make them for myself as an after-school snack, watching them rise through the window in the oven door with a glass of milk in hand, sniffing their fragrance from the oven's output fan. Their soft, pillowy texture and delicate flavor constitute the cookie ideal, in my opinion. They make a fantastic ice cream sandwich cookie, and can be topped with icing for party cookies.

¾ cup sugar

⅔ cup canola oil

2 large eggs

2 teaspoons vanilla extract

¼ teaspoon almond extract

2 cups all-purpose flour

2 teaspoons baking powder

¼ teaspoon kosher salt

Heat the oven to 350°F. Line baking sheets with parchment paper.

In a bowl, whisk together the sugar, oil, eggs, vanilla, and almond extract until smooth. Add the flour, baking powder, and salt and stir until just combined. Using a large tablespoon, drop balls of dough about 2 inches apart onto the prepared baking sheets. Bake, rotating the baking sheets halfway through, until golden brown at the edges, about 10 minutes. Let cool on wire racks.

# Cocoons

We named ours for their resemblance to a caterpillar's home, but elsewhere these buttery delights are known as Mexican wedding cookies, Greek wedding cookies, Russian tea cookies, or Viennese crescents. Whatever you call them, these traditional shortbread cookies studded with chopped nuts and coated in confectioners' sugar are an undisputed holiday classic. My aunt Barbara Jane always used pecans in hers and said that balls were easier to pack into Christmas cookie tins than the traditional crescent shape. You can use any nuts and any shape you like, but I like mine like Barbara Jane's.

14 tablespoons (1¾ sticks) unsalted butter, at room temperature

2¼ cups confectioners' sugar, plus more if desired

1 tablespoon vanilla extract

2 cups all-purpose flour

1 cup finely chopped pecans

1 teaspoon kosher salt

Heat the oven to 325°F. Line a baking sheet with parchment paper.

In a bowl, combine the butter, ¼ cup of the confectioners' sugar, and the vanilla and beat with a handheld mixer on medium-high speed until smooth, pale, and fluffy, about 3 minutes. Add the flour, pecans, and salt and mix until just combined. Using a 1-ounce ice cream scoop or two tablespoons, portion out and shape the dough into 1½-inch-diameter balls. Place the balls 2 inches apart on the prepared baking sheet. Bake until firm and very lightly browned where the cookie touches the parchment, about 30 minutes. Let cool on the pan for about 5 minutes, then transfer to a large bowl, add the remaining 2 cups confectioners' sugar, and toss until evenly coated. Transfer to a wire rack and let cool completely. Repeat with the remaining dough and sugar.

Once these cookies are all cooled, I usually toss them again in confectioners' sugar for a fresh coat, but they're perfectly servable as is.

PICTURED, FROM TOP LEFT:
Pretzel-Peanut-Chocolate Candy (page 191), Cocoons, Crisp Oatmeal Raisin Cookies (page 175)

# Cream Cheese Snickerdoodles

MAKES ABOUT 48 COOKIES

More of an ooey-gooey drug in disk form than a normal cookie, this update on the classic southern recipe is ridiculously overindulgent. But that's okay! Just remember to make these only when you have tons of friends around or for a party. These are perfect paired with fresh vanilla ice cream for sandwiches, too.

3 cups all-purpose flour

2 teaspoons cream of tartar

1 teaspoon baking soda

¼ teaspoon kosher salt

1 (8-ounce) package cream cheese, at room temperature

4 tablespoons (½ stick) unsalted butter, softened

1¾ cups sugar

4 teaspoons ground cinnamon

1½ teaspoons vanilla extract

2 large eggs

Line baking sheets with parchment paper.

In a bowl, whisk together the flour, cream of tartar, baking soda, and salt. Put the cream cheese, butter, 1½ cups of the sugar, 1 teaspoon of the cinnamon, and the vanilla in a bowl and beat with a handheld mixer on medium-high speed until pale and fluffy, about 2 minutes. Add the eggs and beat until smooth. Add the dry ingredients and beat until just combined. Using a 1-ounce ice scream scoop or two tablespoons, portion out the dough and shape each portion into a ball. Roll the balls in the remaining ¼ cup sugar mixed with the remaining 3 teaspoons cinnamon. Place the balls at least 2 inches apart on the prepared baking sheets. Use a ¼-cup measuring cup to press each ball into a flat disk; chill the disks for about 30 minutes.

Heat the oven to 350°F. Bake, rotating the pans halfway through, until set and very lightly browned on the bottom, about 10 minutes.

VARIATION: To make these cookies with ground cardamom instead of cinnamon, halve the amounts used in the dough and the spiced sugar coating.

# Crisp Oatmeal Raisin Cookies

MAKES ABOUT 36 COOKIES

Chocolate chip cookies get all the glory, but give me these oatmeal raisin gems any day. My aunt Barbara Jane made these every Christmas, but nobody else ever knew that because I kept them all for myself. They're unashamedly cinnamon-packed and thin, almost like Florentines, so they're a little crisp and a little chewy. And they make the most delicious ice cream sandwiches paired with rum-raisin ice cream or Buttered Pecan Ice Cream (page 194).

2 cups all-purpose flour

2 teaspoons ground cinnamon

1 teaspoon baking soda

1 cup (2 sticks) unsalted butter

1 cup packed light brown sugar

1 cup granulated sugar

2 large eggs

1½ cups rolled oats, pulsed in a food processor

1 cup raisins

1 teaspoon vanilla extract

Heat the oven to 350°F. Line baking sheets with parchment paper.

In a bowl, whisk together the flour, cinnamon, and baking soda. In the bowl of a stand mixer fitted with the paddle attachment, beat the butter and both sugars on medium-high speed until fluffy and smooth, about 5 minutes. Add the eggs one at a time and beat until they are completely incorporated and the mixture is smooth. Add the flour mixture and beat on low speed until the flour is just absorbed and the dough is smooth. Add the oats, raisins, and vanilla and beat on low speed until just combined. Refrigerate the dough for 30 minutes.

Using a 1-ounce ice cream scoop or your fingers, portion out and shape the dough into 1-inch-diameter balls. Place the balls at least 2 inches apart on the prepared baking sheets. Working with one baking sheet at a time, bake the cookies, rotating halfway through, until golden brown and just set, 10 to 15 minutes. The outside edges should just be slightly darker than the centers.

Let cool on the baking sheet set on a wire rack for about 10 minutes. Using a metal spatula, transfer the cookies to wire rack to cool completely.

PICTURED, FROM TOP LEFT:
Pretzel-Peanut-Chocolate Candy (page 191), Cocoons (page 171),
Crisp Oatmeal Raisin Cookies

# Grapefruit-Blackberry Bars

SERVES 12 TO 16

Let's face it: Grapefruit gets left on the bench when it comes to desserts. But if bakers can take advantage of the bright sourness of lemon and lime to temper sugar's sweetness, why not the pleasant bitterness of grapefruit? Besides, its color is a knockout, especially in these bars, where blackberries mottle the surface and give the grapefruit a fruity sour note to play with.

---

1 cup (2 sticks) unsalted butter, at room temperature

3¾ cups granulated sugar

3 cups all-purpose flour

⅛ teaspoon kosher salt

6 ounces blackberries

1 tablespoon fresh lime juice

1 tablespoon pomegranate juice

2 tablespoons grated grapefruit zest

½ tablespoon grated lemon zest

1 cup fresh grapefruit juice

2 tablespoons fresh lemon juice

6 large eggs

Confectioners' sugar

Heat the oven to 350°F. Spray a 9-by-13-inch baking pan evenly with baking spray.

In a bowl, beat the butter and ½ cup of the granulated sugar with a handheld mixer on medium-high speed until light and fluffy, 2 to 3 minutes. Add 2 cups of the flour and the salt and mix until combined. Transfer the dough to the prepared pan and press it into the pan to cover the bottom and about halfway up the sides. (I place a sheet of plastic wrap on top of the dough and press using that so my hands don't stick to the dough.) Refrigerate the dough for about 30 minutes. Bake until light brown, about 20 minutes. Remove from the oven and let cool slightly.

In a small saucepan, combine the blackberries, ¼ cup of the granulated sugar, the lime juice, and pomegranate juice and bring to a boil over high heat. Cook, stirring occasionally, until thick, about 10 minutes. Remove from the heat and press through a fine-mesh sieve set over a bowl, pressing on the solids to extract all the juice from the berries. Let cool completely. Discard the solids.

In a bowl, whisk together the remaining 3 cups granulated sugar and 1 cup flour (this is to prevent lumps of flour from forming in the filling), then add the grapefruit and lemon zests, grapefruit and lemon juices, and the eggs and whisk until smooth. Pour the filling onto the crust, then drizzle the blackberry sauce in stripes over the top. Drag a toothpick or knife through the filling and sauce to create swirls. Bake until the filling is just set in the middle but still slightly jiggly in the center, about 35 minutes. Let cool completely at room temperature, then refrigerate for at least 4 hours to set the filling before cutting into bars.

# Strawberry Bars

SERVES 12 TO 16

I've always loved Jell-O salads—especially my aunt's cranberry version over pretzels, which she'd bring to our Thanksgiving table, and my grandmother's strawberry version with a sour cream layer underneath. This bar is best served chilled, so the layers have time to set up, but also to give the strawberry and cream filling a fresh effect when you bite into it, crunching on the salty pretzels underneath.

FOR THE CRUST:

1 cup ground pretzels, plus 1 cup roughly broken pretzel pieces

⅓ cup sugar

½ cup (2 sticks) unsalted butter, melted and cooled

FOR THE CREAM CHEESE LAYER:

2 (8-ounce) packages cream cheese

1 cup sugar

½ teaspoon kosher salt

FOR THE STRAWBERRY LAYER:

1⅔ cups sugar

¼ cup all-purpose flour

Grated zest of ½ orange

½ teaspoon kosher salt

5 large eggs, at room temperature

1¼ cups pureed strawberries (1 pound)

FOR GARNISH:

Confectioners' sugar

1 pound strawberries, hulled and sliced

MAKE THE CRUST: Heat the oven to 350°F. Spray a 9-by-13-inch baking pan evenly with baking spray and then line it with a strip of parchment paper that overhangs on two sides of the pan.

Put the ground pretzels, sugar, and butter in a food processor and process until finely ground and smooth. Stir in the broken pretzel pieces until evenly distributed, then pour into the prepared pan, pressing the mixture evenly over the bottom of the pan to form a compact crust. Bake until the crust begins to brown at the edges and looks slightly dry, about 20 minutes. Let cool completely.

MAKE THE CREAM CHEESE LAYER: In a bowl, beat the cream cheese, sugar, and salt with a handheld mixer on medium-high speed until just smooth, about 1 minute. Pour over the crust and spread evenly to cover it completely. Refrigerate the pan while you make the strawberry layer.

MAKE THE STRAWBERRY LAYER: In a bowl, whisk together the sugar, flour, orange zest, and salt until evenly incorporated. Add the eggs and whisk until smooth, trying not to incorporate too much air. Add the strawberry puree and whisk until smooth. Gently pour the strawberry filling over the cream cheese mixture. Lower the oven temperature to 325°F and bake until the strawberry layer is just set (it shouldn't jiggle at all), 20 to 25 minutes. Let cool completely to room temperature, then refrigerate until chilled, at least 4 hours or overnight.

When ready to serve, use the parchment paper to lift the whole sheet of bars out of the pan and onto a cutting board. Cut into bars but leave them arranged together. Dust the top with confectioners' sugar and then arrange sliced strawberries over the top of the bars in whatever way you like. Separate the bars and serve chilled.

# Vegan Brownies

MAKES 24 BROWNIES

When I first had a taste of a vegan brownie, made with coconut oil and applesauce in place of eggs and butter, it was a revelation. The oil and applesauce achieve that perfectly fudgy brownie texture handily. I adapted my favorite classic brownie recipe and came up with exactly what I think a brownie should be: dark, intensely chocolaty, and moist throughout.

1 cup coconut oil

1 cup applesauce

1 cup granulated cane sugar

1 cup firmly packed dark brown sugar

8 ounces bittersweet chocolate, melted and cooled

2 teaspoons vanilla extract

1½ teaspoons kosher salt

1 cup all-purpose flour

Heat the oven to 350°F. Spray a 9-by-13-inch baking pan evenly with baking spray.

In a large bowl, combine the oil, applesauce, granulated sugar, and brown sugar and whisk until smooth. Add the chocolate, vanilla, and salt and whisk until smooth. Add the flour and whisk vigorously for about 1 minute, until smooth and all the ingredients are evenly incorporated. Pour the batter into the prepared baking pan and smooth the top with a rubber spatula. Bake until a toothpick inserted in the middle of the brownies comes out clean, about 45 minutes.

Let cool completely before cutting into squares and serving. If you try to cut them while even slightly warm, I promise you'll be eating pudding instead of a solid bar—which, come to think of it, is not so bad. Choose your fate!

# Buckeyes

(PEANUT BUTTER–CREAM CHEESE BALLS DIPPED IN CHOCOLATE)

MAKES ABOUT 30 CONFECTIONS

One of my earliest memories is of a show-and-tell day in my prekindergarten class. I had to bring in something from home, and my dad sent me to school with buckeyes from his buckeye tree out in our backyard. I didn't even know what they were, and maybe that's why my presentation fell flat, but I know now that if I'd brought these confections instead, I'd have been the hit of the class. Traditionally peanut butter and cream cheese rolled into balls and then dipped in chocolate, they're very simple but hit all the right notes flavor-wise, as perfect a treat after school as in a holiday tin.

1 (8-ounce) package cream cheese, softened

½ cup smooth peanut butter

4 tablespoons (½ stick) unsalted butter, softened

2 cups confectioners' sugar, sifted

1 teaspoon vanilla extract

½ teaspoon kosher salt

8 ounces bittersweet chocolate, melted

Put the cream cheese in a bowl and beat with a handheld mixer on medium speed until smooth. Add the peanut butter and butter and beat until smooth. Add the confectioners' sugar, vanilla, and salt and beat until very smooth and lightened, about 2 minutes. Refrigerate the dough until firm, about 1 hour. Using a 1-ounce ice cream scoop or two tablespoons, portion out the dough and shape into 1-inch balls, rolling them in your hands to smooth their surface; refrigerate again until set.

Place a chilled ball on a fork, and use the fork to dip the ball into the chocolate, leaving the top third exposed. Lift the fork, letting the excess chocolate drain back into the bowl, then carefully slide the ball onto a sheet of parchment or wax paper, using another fork or knife to push it gently off the first fork. Repeat until all the balls are coated, then refrigerate the balls to harden the chocolate. Serve the balls chilled or at room temperature.

NOTE: Because the chocolate is not tempered here, it will "bloom," a technical term for the chocolate that hasn't been properly melted, resulting in a spotty, streaky appearance when it hardens. It does not affect the taste of the chocolate and will show up only after a day or so. It doesn't bother me, since most candies I make aren't going to last longer than a couple hours after they're served, and as long as you keep these candies refrigerated, you'll have no problems at all.

# Buttermilk Caramels

MAKES 64 CANDIES

I've always loved chewy caramel candies, but most of them are little more than sugar and corn syrup. I wanted to develop a recipe that has a more grown-up character. Tangy buttermilk lightens the candies and adds a sophisticated sourness to the burnished treats. Lyle's golden syrup (see page 113) adds a buttery lusciousness that, along with the sea salt's saline crunch, takes these caramels truly over the top.

1¼ cups buttermilk

1 cup sugar

½ cup Lyle's golden syrup

½ cup (1 stick) unsalted butter

Coarse sea salt

Line the bottom of an 8-inch square baking pan with parchment paper and spray the paper evenly with baking spray.

In a medium-size saucepan, heat the buttermilk, sugar, and syrup over medium heat, stirring until the sugar dissolves, about 5 minutes. Bring to a boil and attach a candy thermometer to the side of the pan; cook, without stirring, until the mixture reaches 260°F, about 45 minutes. Remove the pan from the heat and stir in the butter until smooth.

Pour the sugar mixture into the prepared baking pan and sprinkle the top evenly with salt. Let cool completely, about 8 hours, then cut into small squares to serve. Wrap any leftovers in wax or parchment paper squares to give as gifts.

# Marbled Chocolate Bark

WITH NUTS AND DRIED FRUITS

SERVES 16 TO 20

Holidays just aren't the same without chocolate bark. I especially love the peppermint and white chocolate versions that you find in virtually every specialty food store in the country around the end of the year. In this version, I use good-quality chocolate and natural ingredients like toasted nuts and dried fruits to make it a substantial holiday snack. Because it's full of nuts and fruits (think of it as trail mix with a little more chocolate), you don't have to feel guilty about eating sheets of it around the holidays like I do. It makes the perfect homemade gift for stocking stuffers or party favors, too. Feel free to mix up the ingredients with whatever you have on hand or suits your tastes; the possibilities for variations are endless.

---

8 ounces good-quality bittersweet chocolate, chopped

8 ounces good-quality white chocolate, chopped

½ cup sliced Brazil nuts

½ cup cashews

½ cup toasted pumpkin seeds

½ cup dried cranberries

½ cup toasted shaved coconut

Put the dark chocolate and white chocolate in separate heatproof bowls. Bring a small saucepan of water to a simmer. Place one bowl of chocolate over the pan (make sure the bottom of the bowl doesn't actually touch the water) and stir often until the chocolate is fully melted. Remove the pan and let cool for a few minutes while you melt the other chocolate in the same way.

Once both chocolates are melted and cooled for 5 to 10 minutes, line a large baking sheet that will fit in your refrigerator with parchment or wax paper. Pour the chocolates on the paper, either in rows or blobs, until they form a somewhat cohesive shape. Using a toothpick, swirl the chocolates into each other to create a spiral effect. Sprinkle the chocolate with the nuts, seeds, cranberries, and coconut and refrigerate until set. When you're ready to serve it, break the bark into bite-size pieces.

# Chocolate-Covered Mints

MAKES ABOUT 36 CANDIES

When I was growing up in Mississippi, my family would eat out weekly at the Carmack Fish House, a local fried-catfish joint about a mile away from where my grandmother lived in Carmack. Despite the temptation of a soft-serve ice cream machine, the only dessert I wanted after the buffet was a single, cooling Pearson's mint patty. I'd pluck one from the plastic jug on my way out the door and hear my father tell the cashier, "Four buffet dinners, and one of those mints." This homemade version is super simple to make and just as delicious as those Pearson's mints. And now I can have them whenever I want, without having to smell like fried catfish for days afterward. Note that this candy contains a raw egg white, so be sure to use a very fresh one.

---

1 large egg white, at room temperature

1 teaspoon fresh lemon juice

½ teaspoon peppermint extract (see Note)

1 (1-pound) box confectioners' sugar, plus more for the work surface if needed

8 ounces bittersweet chocolate, melted

Line a baking sheet with parchment paper.

In a large bowl, whisk the egg white and lemon juice until frothy and loose, but not to the point where it develops peaks. Add the peppermint extract and confectioners' sugar and slowly stir with a fork until a dough forms. You will have to take the dough out of the bowl near the end of mixing and start kneading by hand, but all the sugar will become incorporated. Once the dough is smooth, either break off walnut-size chunks, roll them into balls, then flatten them, or roll the entire mass of dough out on a confectioners' sugar–dusted work surface with a rolling pin until ¼ inch thick and cut out 1¼-inch rounds with a cookie cutter, until you have about 36 mints. Place them on the prepared baking sheet and let them sit to dry out for about 4 hours.

When the mints are dry on the surface, use two forks to carefully dip each mint in the chocolate to coat, then return it to the baking sheet. Refrigerate the chocolate-covered mints until the chocolate sets. Serve chilled.

NOTE: To vary the flavor of these confections, simply substitute another extract in a flavor you like. Orange, raspberry, and strawberry all make great pairings with chocolate, but play around to make your version all your own.

# Pretzel-Peanut-Chocolate Candy

MAKES ABOUT 24 CANDIES

A recipe for candy with three ingredients? Why, yes, if only because it is the most satisfying morsel I've ever eaten in one sitting. Every year at Christmastime, at least once, I sit and gorge myself on the sweet, salty, crunchy until I ruin my supper . . . and still go back for more.

1¼ pounds bittersweet chocolate, finely chopped

6 ounces stick pretzels, lightly crushed

6 ounces roasted salted peanuts

Put the chocolate in a medium-size heatproof bowl. Bring a medium-size saucepan of water to a simmer. Place the bowl of chocolate over the pan (make sure the bottom of the bowl doesn't actually touch the water) and stir often until the chocolate is almost fully melted. Remove from the heat and continue to stir until completely melted. Add the pretzels and peanuts and stir until evenly coated in the chocolate.

Using two spoons, drop large spoonfuls of the chocolate-covered peanuts and pretzels onto a sheet of aluminum foil and let cool completely until hardened. Store in an airtight container for up to 3 days or in the refrigerator for up to 1 week.

# Frozen Treats

BUTTERED PECAN ICE CREAM

CHERRY-LIME SORBET

CREAM CHEESE SORBET

LEMON CURD–VANILLA SWIRL ICE CREAM

OLD-FASHIONED PEACH ICE CREAM

SPICE ICE CREAM

VANILLA SOFT-SERVE

COLA GRANITA

# Buttered Pecan Ice Cream

MAKES ABOUT 1½ QUARTS

The pecan is the greatest nut in existence, in my opinion. No matter what ice cream shop I'd go to as a kid, no matter what other new or irresistible flavors they had, if there was buttered pecan, that's what I got. Its creamy, salty, sweet goldenness just can't be beat.

½ cup (1 stick) unsalted butter

2 cups whole pecan halves

¼ cup packed light brown sugar

1 large egg white, lightly beaten

4 large egg yolks

1 cup granulated sugar

½ teaspoon kosher salt

2 cups milk

1 cup heavy cream

1 tablespoon vanilla extract

Heat the oven to 350°F. Line a baking sheet with aluminum foil.

Put the butter in a 12-inch skillet and cook over medium heat, stirring often, until the butter begins to brown and smell nutty, 3 to 5 minutes. Add the pecans, toss them in the butter until evenly coated, and cook until they are toasted and have absorbed most of the butter. Pour into a bowl and let cool completely.

In a medium-size bowl, combine the brown sugar and egg white and whisk until slightly frothy and smooth (the sugar will not dissolve completely). Add the cooled pecans and stir until evenly coated. Pour onto the prepared baking sheet and spread into an even layer, separating the nuts so none are touching. Bake until the sugar mixture is dried on the outside of the pecans, tossing them halfway through, about 10 minutes. Let cool completely, then break the nuts apart. Store at room temperature in an airtight container for up to 1 week, or until you're ready to use them.

In a medium-size saucepan, whisk together the egg yolks, granulated sugar, and salt until smooth and light, at least 1 minute. Add the milk and whisk until smooth. Place over medium heat and cook, stirring often with a heatproof spatula, until the mixture thickens slightly and coats the back of a spoon (you'll also know the custard is almost ready when the foam on the surface disappears and the mixture stops moving abruptly after giving it a quick stir). Remove from the heat and pour through a fine-mesh sieve into a bowl. Add the cream and vanilla and stir until smooth. Refrigerate the custard until chilled, at least 2 hours.

Pour the chilled custard into an ice cream maker and freeze according to the manufacturer's instructions. When the ice cream looks perfectly churned, add the candied pecans to the machine and let them mix into the ice cream. Transfer to a resealable plastic container and freeze until firm, at least 4 hours, before serving.

# Cherry-Lime Sorbet

### MAKES ABOUT 1½ QUARTS

I set out to re-create the taste of Sonic's cherry limeade with this sorbet. It was my favorite drink in the summertime, and now that I no longer have access to it because there are none of those iconic drive-through restaurants near me, this sweet and tangy sorbet does just the trick. It also makes good use of fresh sour cherries, which are around only for a couple weeks and gone before you know it.

---

1 pound fresh or thawed frozen
   sour cherries, pitted

1 cup sugar

½ teaspoon kosher salt

Finely grated zest of 1 lime

¼ cup fresh lime juice

2 tablespoons kirsch (cherry brandy)

In a medium-size saucepan, combine the cherries, sugar, and salt and mash with a potato masher or wooden spoon until the sugar is soaked in cherry juice. Place the pan over medium heat and cook, stirring, until the sugar dissolves. Remove from the heat and add ¾ cup water, the lime zest, lime juice, and kirsch. Pour into a blender and puree until smooth. Pour through a fine-mesh sieve into a bowl, pressing on the solids to extract as much of the liquid as possible, then cover with plastic wrap and refrigerate until chilled, at least 2 hours or up to 3 days. Discard the solids, or save them for another use.

Pour the chilled liquid into an ice cream maker and freeze according to the manufacturer's instructions. Transfer to a resealable plastic container and freeze until firm, at least 4 hours, before serving. Because sorbets have no dairy fat, they are rock hard when frozen solid. To make your life easier, remove the sorbet from the freezer about 10 minutes before serving to let it soften slightly. Or, better yet, churn the sorbet while eating dinner and serve it fresh from the ice cream maker.

# Cream Cheese Sorbet

MAKES 1 QUART

If you're like me and love cream cheese but feel like you need to run a marathon after most desserts made with it, then this sorbet is for you. Yes, I know it's not technically a sorbet because the cream cheese itself is a dairy product, but it's made like sorbet with no additional dairy or egg yolks. A tart lime-infused simple syrup, vanilla, and salt round out and balance the pure cream cheese flavor.

4 (8-ounce) packages
    cream cheese, softened

2 cups sugar

2 cups purified water

½ teaspoon kosher salt

½ cup fresh lime juice

1½ teaspoons vanilla extract

Put the cream cheese in a large bowl and beat with a handheld mixer on medium-high speed until smooth. In a small saucepan, bring the sugar, water, and salt to a boil, stirring, until the sugar is dissolved. Remove from the heat and slowly drizzle the syrup into the cream cheese while beating so that you avoid creating any lumps. Stir in the juice and vanilla until smooth, then refrigerate for at least 1 hour.

Pour into an ice cream maker and freeze according to the manufacturer's instructions. Serve right away while soft or transfer to a resealable plastic container and freeze until firm, at least 4 hours, before serving.

# Lemon Curd–Vanilla Swirl Ice Cream

MAKES ABOUT 1½ QUARTS

I created this recipe for an ice cream–making contest in Brooklyn a few years ago. Since my favorite dessert is a pavlova, I decided to spin that idea and serve an ice cream surrounded by crunchy meringue bits and fresh fruit. Lemon curd is the traditional sauce for a pavlova, so I marbled it into a very egg yolk–rich ice cream base. Luckily, one of the judges was an Aussie, an owner of Van Leeuwen Artisan Ice Cream, and thus had a soft spot for pavlova, but it was the amount of egg yolks in the recipe that won it for me. The egg yolks contribute a luxurious velvety mouthfeel to the ice cream.

## FOR THE LEMON CURD:

¾ cup sugar

8 large egg yolks

2 teaspoons grated lemon zest

¾ cup fresh lemon juice

¾ cup (1½ sticks) cold unsalted butter, cut into ½-inch cubes

## FOR THE ICE CREAM:

½ cup sugar

½ teaspoon kosher salt

5 large egg yolks

½ vanilla bean, split, seeds scraped and reserved

2 cups milk

¾ cup heavy cream

1½ teaspoons vanilla extract

**MAKE THE LEMON CURD:** In a small saucepan, whisk together the sugar and egg yolks until smooth and light; add the lemon zest and lemon juice and mix until smooth. Place the pan over medium heat and cook, stirring often with a heatproof spatula, until thickened to the consistency of loose pudding, about 10 minutes. Remove from the heat and gradually whisk in the butter, letting each cube incorporate before adding the next. Transfer the curd to a bowl and press a piece of plastic wrap directly onto the surface; poke holes through the plastic wrap to allow steam to escape. Let cool to room temperature, then refrigerate until chilled, at least 2 hours.

**MAKE THE ICE CREAM:** In a medium-size saucepan, whisk together the sugar, salt, egg yolks, and vanilla seeds until smooth and light, at least 1 minute. Add the milk and whisk until smooth. Place over medium heat and cook, stirring often with a heatproof spatula, until the mixture thickens slightly and coats the back of a spoon (you'll also know the custard is almost ready when the foam on the surface disappears and the mixture stops moving abruptly after giving it a quick stir). Pour through a fine-mesh sieve into a bowl. Add the cream and vanilla and stir until smooth. Refrigerate the custard until chilled, at least 2 hours.

Pour the chilled custard into an ice cream maker and freeze according to the manufacturer's instructions. Transfer to a resealable plastic container, alternating layers of it with the chilled lemon curd. Using a table knife, swirl the layers together and around to create a rippled effect. Cover and place in the freezer until firm, at least 4 hours, before serving.

# Old-Fashioned Peach Ice Cream

MAKES ABOUT 1½ QUARTS

The thought of peach ice cream still conjures childhood memories of staring at an old-fashioned crank-style ice cream maker while the canister of cream spun and spun in a sea of rock salt and my arm nearly fell off from exhaustion. I use schnapps here to intensify the peach flavor, but make sure you use one from an artisanal maker so as not to dilute the peach flavor with artificial syrup. If you can't get your hands on good-quality schnapps, just omit it and wait until your peaches are so perfectly ripe as to be almost falling apart. Their pure flavor alone will more than suffice here.

---

1 pound fresh or thawed frozen peaches, peeled, pitted, and finely chopped

2 tablespoons good-quality peach schnapps

4 large egg yolks

1 cup sugar

½ teaspoon kosher salt

2 cups whole milk

1 cup heavy cream

Put half of the peaches and 1 tablespoon of the schnapps in a 12-inch skillet and cook over medium-low heat, stirring often, until fragrant and the peaches just start sticking to the pan. Remove from the heat and stir in the remaining peaches and remaining 1 tablespoon schnapps; let cool completely.

In a medium-size saucepan, whisk together the egg yolks, sugar, and salt until smooth and light, at least 1 minute. Add the milk and whisk until smooth. Place over medium heat and cook, stirring often with a heatproof spatula, until the mixture thickens slightly and coats the back of a spoon (you'll also know the custard is almost ready when the foam on the surface disappears and the mixture stops moving abruptly after giving it a quick stir). Remove from the heat and pour through a fine-mesh sieve into a bowl. Add the peaches and cream and stir until smooth. Refrigerate the custard until chilled, at least 2 hours.

Pour the chilled custard into an ice cream maker and freeze according to the manufacturer's instructions. Transfer to a resealable plastic container and freeze until firm, at least 4 hours, before serving.

# Spice Ice Cream

MAKES ABOUT 1½ QUARTS

When I first developed a nutmeg ice cream for *Saveur* years ago, it was a bigger hit than I thought it would ever be—an ideal thrifty dessert, it used up all those small leftover nutmeg nubs you end up with after grating it fresh. For this book, I wanted an ice cream that didn't taste just of nutmeg but featured all the warm winter spices. They work together to make a pleasing, aromatic ice cream that's ideal served over apple pie, bread pudding, or Pecan Pie (page 90).

2 cups milk

1 vanilla bean, split, seeds scraped and reserved

1 cinnamon stick

½ star anise pod

4 whole cloves

4 allspice berries

1 broken nutmeg pod or 3 to 4 nub ends

1 (1-inch) piece fresh ginger, peeled and thinly sliced

4 large egg yolks

1 cup sugar

½ teaspoon kosher salt

1 cup heavy cream

In a small saucepan, combine the milk, vanilla bean and seeds, cinnamon, star anise, cloves, allspice, nutmeg, and ginger. Bring to a boil, then immediately remove from the heat, cover, and let sit to infuse with the spices' strong flavor for about 1 hour.

In a medium-size saucepan, whisk together the egg yolks, sugar, and salt until smooth and light, at least 1 minute. Add the spiced milk (including the vanilla bean, spices, and ginger) and whisk well. Place over medium heat and cook, stirring often with a heatproof spatula, until the mixture thickens slightly and coats the back of a spoon (you'll also know the custard is almost ready when the foam on the surface disappears and the mixture stops moving abruptly after giving it a quick stir). Remove from the heat and pour through a fine-mesh sieve into a bowl; discard the solids. Add the cream and stir until smooth. Refrigerate the custard until chilled, at least 2 hours.

Pour the chilled custard into an ice cream maker and freeze according to the manufacturer's instructions. Transfer to a resealable plastic container and freeze until firm, at least 4 hours, before serving.

# Vanilla Soft-Serve

MAKES ABOUT 1½ QUARTS

Once you've had fresh, soft vanilla ice cream straight from the churn, there's really no going back to the store-bought variety. The pillowy soft texture and layered aroma of vanilla from the fresh-churned cream are incredible. I implore you to make this ice cream, but don't churn it until right before you serve it; you won't be sorry. Try it with chopped fresh fruit or a big spoonful of Cola Granita (page 208).

4 large egg yolks

1 cup sugar

½ teaspoon kosher salt

1 vanilla bean, split,
   seeds scraped and reserved

2 cups milk

1 cup heavy cream

1 tablespoon vanilla extract

In a medium-size saucepan, whisk together the egg yolks, sugar, salt, and vanilla seeds and bean until smooth and light, at least 1 minute. Add the milk and whisk well. Place over medium heat and cook, stirring often with a heatproof spatula, until the mixture thickens slightly and coats the back of a spoon (you'll also know the custard is almost ready when the foam on the surface disappears and the mixture stops moving abruptly after giving it a quick stir). Pour through a fine-mesh sieve into a bowl. Add the cream and vanilla and stir until smooth. Refrigerate the custard until chilled, at least 2 hours.

Pour the chilled custard into an ice cream maker and freeze according to the manufacturer's directions. When the ice cream looks perfectly churned, call your friends over and immediately scoop the soft ice cream into chilled bowls and eat it right away. Of course, if you want, you can pour the ice cream into a resealable plastic container and freeze until firm, at least 4 hours, before serving.

# Cola Granita

SERVES 4 TO 6

Now, bear with me in the cooking method here. It may seem strange to reduce a can of soda and then stir it into another, but I've always found two things to be true when freezing sorbets and other watery syrups: One, because they're served colder, the flavors need to be super intense, since cold numbs your taste buds and also prohibits flavor compounds from blossoming to their fullest potential. And two, when you freeze a soda, it ends up just tasting watery. So, here, I reduce some of the soda, removing excess water to reveal something like its original syrup, then stir it into more soda, intensifying the flavor.

---

4 cups cola

½ cup sugar

1 teaspoon kosher salt

2 tablespoons fresh lime juice

1 teaspoon vanilla extract

In a 2-quart saucepan, combine 1 cup of the cola, the sugar, and salt and cook over medium-high heat, stirring, until the sugar is dissolved. Remove from the heat and stir in the remaining 3 cups cola, the lime juice, and vanilla; let cool.

Pour into an 8-inch square baking dish and place in the freezer. Freeze, scraping and stirring the mixture thoroughly every hour to prevent it from freezing into a solid mass, until the mixture is the consistency of shaved ice, about 4 hours. Spoon into chilled bowls to serve.

PICTURED, OPPOSITE:
Cola Granita atop Vanilla Soft-Serve (page 206)

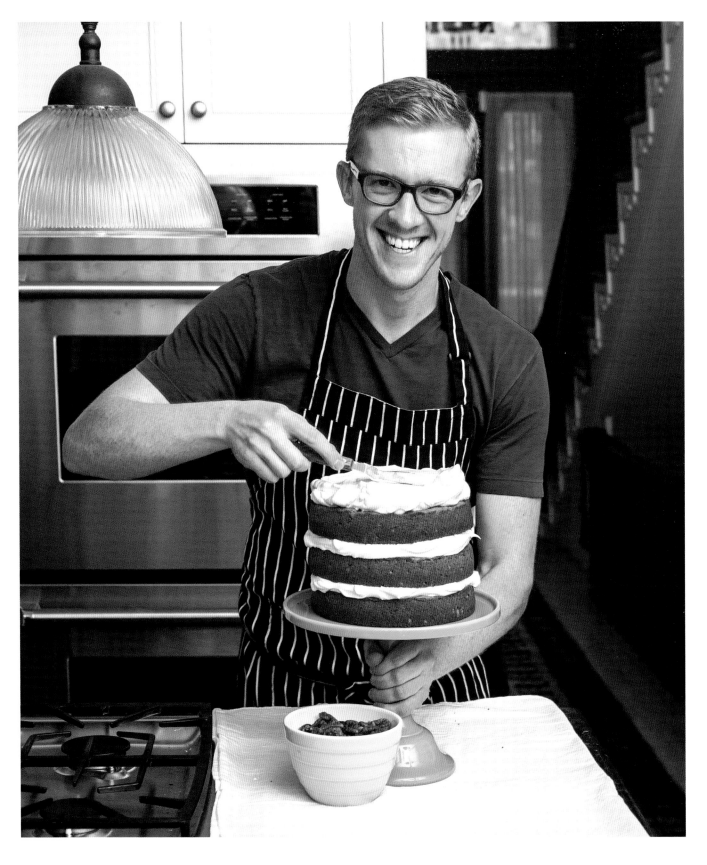

# Acknowledgments

To my mother and father, aunt Barbara Jane, grandmother Carol, and countless other friends, family, and southern cooks who've given me recipes, fed me graciously, or imparted their culinary wisdom onto me over the years—thank you. To everyone I worked with at *Saveur* for six years whom I consider true friends: Dana Bowen, Katie Cancilla, Todd Coleman, Kellie Evans, Greg Ferro, Georgia Freedman-Wand, Gabriella Gershenson, Dorothy Irwin, Sarah Karnasiewicz, Beth Kracklauer, Hunter Lewis, Dave McAninch, Marne Setton, Karen Shimizu, Judith Sonntag, and, especially, Betsy Andrews and James Oseland, whose combined efforts helped me write the essay that lit the spark for this book—thank you. To my mentors and teachers in the industry, Arlyn Blake, Pichet Ong, and Nick Malgieri—thank you for the shared wisdom and advice.

Jono Jarrett, thank you for sending me the e-mail that changed my life and for shepherding me through this whole process with grace and hilarious one-liners. To Noah Fecks, thank you for the gorgeous photographs and entertaining stories that have me laughing to this day. To Paul Wagtouicz and Jenn Kim, thank you for the support during the shoot, and Keith Marran and David Reich (and Oz and Gogo), thank you for your beautiful home and generous hospitality.

# Index